IDIOMS IN THE BIBLE EXPLAINED
AND
A KEY TO THE ORIGINAL GOSPEL

BY THE AUTHOR

Holy Bible From the Ancient Eastern Text
Old Testament Light

Idioms in the Bible Explained

and

A Key to the Original Gospel

GEORGE M. LAMSA

HarperOne
An Imprint of HarperCollins*Publishers*

HarperOne

Originally published separately as *Idioms in the Bible Explained* and *Key to Original Gospels*

HarperCollins books may be purchased for educational, business, or sales promotional use. For information, please e-mail the Special Markets Department at SPsales@harpercollins.com.

HarperCollins Web site: http://www.harpercollins.com

HarperCollins®, 📖®, and HarperOne™ are trademarks of HarperCollins Publishers.

Library of Congress Cataloging-in-Publication Data

Lamsa, George Mamishisho.
    Idioms in the Bible explained; and, A key to the original Gospels.

    Second work originally published under title: Key to original Gospels.
      1. Bible—Language style. 2. Bible. N.T. Gospels—Criticism, interpretation, etc.
    I. Lamsa, George Mamishisho. Key to original Gospels. 1985. II. Title: Idioms in the
    Bible explained.   III. Title: Key to the original Gospels.
    BS537.L35   1985
    220.4   85–42782
    ISBN: 978–0–06–064927–2

24 25 26 27 28 LBC 59 58 57 56 55

Contents

Part One:
Idioms in the Bible Explained

Part Two:
A Key to the Original Gospel

Introduction

All languages of the world, both ancient and modern, have idioms, metaphors and mannerisms of speech. This style of speech is called colloquialism. An idiom is a saying that foreigners cannot understand without being trained and is often taken literally and therefore misunderstood. This is because when we use an idiom we say one thing, but we mean another. For example, in Aramaic we say, "If your hand offends you, cut it off," which means, "If you have a habit of stealing, cut it out." An English idiom, "He is in a pickle," really means, "He is in trouble." Therefore, idioms and colloquialisms are not to be taken literally. A student must know their true meanings in order to translate them accurately into another language.

Idioms, metaphors and figures of speech constitute a great barrier in mastering a foreign language. Translators from one language into another have always been cognizant of these difficulties. This is one reason why the Bible is misunderstood and has been subjected to revision throughout the centuries. The sixteenth century translators of the Holy Bible did not understand the idioms of the languages from which they translated. Therefore they translated idioms literally and their true meanings were lost. This is not all, they were also unfamiliar with the Eastern customs and manners which constitute the background of the Bible. All the authors of the Bible were born and reared in the East, and they spoke the Semitic languages of Aramaic and Hebrew.

Invariably, people throughout the world think and express themselves differently. Moreover, their customs and manners are varied. Nevertheless, what they say in their own language is well-understood by their own people. But, when translated into an alien tongue, many words and phrases lose their meanings completely and others are obscured. These varied differences in speech cannot be learned by the means of text books or dictionaries. One has to live with an alien people in order to understand their idioms and mannerisms of speech.

Years ago I was surprised to read in a newspaper that a U.S. navy yard was *firing* twenty-five hundred workers because they had no jobs for them. My little pocket dictionary stated, *"Fire:* to shoot; to set on fire." This idiom horrified me whenever I came across it. I also did not understand the use of the word, "fresh," such as "fresh food," and "a fresh man." The word "fair" was confusing too, such as, "a fair judge," and "a fair woman."

Today, thousands of foreign students in our colleges and universities are puzzled just as I was when they come across some of the American idioms and colloquialisms with so many meanings. For example, "He has been an underdog;" "He was born with a silver spoon in his mouth;" "He is in a jam;" "He is in hot water;" "To give the bride a shower." In the East, brides are bathed before the nuptials. I thought the Americans had the same custom as in the Holy Land. When a lady invited me to her apartment and said, "We will have a shower," I said, "No thank you, I always take my bath in the morning."

There are about five-hundred words in the English language which have more than five-thousand meanings. Now if English, which is a comparatively modern language, has so many idioms and words with different meanings, then we must realize that ancient languages have more idioms than English, and are much more difficult to understand. As an example, a man said to Jesus, "Let me bury my father." This expression means, "Let me first take care of my father until he dies." But foreign scholars took it for granted that this man's father was dead and that Jesus was not interested in his burial. Such an ancient idiom is still used in Eastern languages everyday and is easily understood, even by the common and illiterate people. Also, in Philemon 1:18, we read that Paul told Philemon, one of his converts, to receive back his servant who had stolen some money from him and had run away. Paul wrote to him, "Whatever he owes you, put it on my account," which in Aramaic means, "Forget it," or as Americans say in English, "Put it on the cuff." Western commentators have portrayed Philemon as the world's first banker from whom Paul borrowed money. This idiom is still used daily in several languages in the Middle East. Paul tells Philemon that he owes him a great deal because he had converted him to Christ.

As I have said before, students of a foreign language take every word exactly as written. They do not know which is an idiom and which is not an idiom. The English idiom, "A man born with a silver spoon in his mouth," would be taken literally by Easterners to mean, "Being born miraculously."

The author of this book, while translating the Holy Scriptures from the ancient Aramaic language into English, became cognizant of the importance of the idioms and metaphors of the Bible. Therefore, he compiled nearly one-thousand idioms from the Scriptures to facilitate the reading and understanding of the Holy Bible. It must be remembered that just as Shakespeare, Milton and Browning wrote for the English-speaking people, so Moses, the prophets and the apostles wrote to their own people. They used their own idioms and metaphors, which were well-understood and still are understood in their original context.

I am sure this volume will be of great assistance to readers of the Holy Bible, regardless of their religious affiliation. The idioms translated in this book will help to elucidate hundreds of obscure and obtuse passages and make the Word of God so plain that even simple people will understand it. God commanded the prophets to write in a plain language so that the unlearned people might understand His Word.

Deut. 27:8, "And you shall write upon the stones all the words of this law very plainly." (Eastern Text—Lamsa)

Hab. 2:2, "And the Lord answered me and said, Write the vision, and make it plain upon tablets, that he who reads it may understand it clearly." (Eastern Text—Lamsa)

The author of this book, and the translator of the Holy Bible from Aramaic into English, was born and reared in a region in the near East which had escaped modernization, a region where the customs, manners and idioms of the ancient Aramaic language are still miraculously preserved to the present day. The language did not change because the area remained remote and isolated until World War II. Aramaic was the *lingua franca* of what is known as the Fertile Crescent, from time immemorial until the thirteenth century, when Aramaic was replaced by a sister tongue, Arabic. This fact is well known.

I chose the King James text from which to pick the idioms quoted in this book (unless otherwise indicated), because the King James text is the most widely used Bible translation in the English speaking world. Moreover, the King James translators were more faithful to the texts from which they translated into English, making fewer additions and omissions than later English version translators and revisors. They translated many Eastern idioms and metaphors literally, not knowing their true meaning. For instance, "You shall handle snakes." They did not know that the word "snake" refers to "an enemy." "Beware of dogs" was not understood to be "beware of gossipers," in Semitic languages.

Most of the idioms in this book have been explained in my translation of the Bible from the Aramaic and the commentaries thereon. I believe the following idiom translations facilitate the reading of the Bible, whether it be the King James or other English versions. Since millions of people have yet to become acquainted with my translation and my commentaries, this volume will be helpful to them.

The author is grateful to Robert James Heinecamp, a student of his, for the help in compiling these idioms.

May the Lord God bless those who search for His truth which endures forever and those who use this little volume as a key to eludicate many of the difficulties in the Book of Books.

Many of the idioms explained in this book can be found in the author's translation of the Holy Bible from the Aramaic published by A. J. Holman Company, Philadelphia, Pennsylvania.

Part One

Idioms in the Bible Explained

THE BOOK OF GENESIS

Let there be light. Gen. 1:3
> *Let there be enlightenment; let there be understanding.*

Darkness. Gen. 1:4
> *Ignorance; lack of enlightenment and understanding.*

Eden. Gen. 2:8
> *A delightful place; temporal life.*

Garden. Gen. 2:8
> *Metaphorically—a wife; a family.*

Tree of life in the midst of the garden. Gen. 2:9
> *Sex; posterity, progeny.*

The tree of the knowledge of good and evil. Gen. 2:9
> *Moral law; the knowledge of good and evil.*

The tree of life. Gen. 2:9
> *Eternal life.*

The tree of good and evil. Gen. 2:17
> *Metaphorically—sexual relationship.*

Good. Gen. 2:17
> *Anything perfect.*

Evil. Gen. 2:17
> *Anything imperfect; contrary to good; immature.*

Naked. Gen. 2:25
> *Exposed; ashamed.*

Serpent. Gen. 3:1
> *An enemy; deception.*

Thorns and thistles. Gen. 3:18
> *Grievances and difficulties.*

Sent forth from the garden. Gen. 3:23
A loss of harmony; a lost paradise.

God took him away. Gen. 5:24
He died painlessly. He had a heart attack.

Sons of God. Gen. 6:2
Good men; the descendants of Seth.

My spirit shall not dwell in man forever. Gen. 6:3
I have become weary and impatient. (A scribal note.)

The Lord was sorry that He made man. Gen. 6:6
(A scribal note. See Old Testament Light—Lamsa.)

I set my bow in the clouds. Gen. 9:13
I set the rainbow in the sky.

I have lifted up my hands. Gen. 14:22
I am taking a solemn oath.

Thy seed. Gen. 17:7
Your offspring; your teaching.

Angels. Gen. 19:1
God's counsel; spirits; God's thoughts.

Looking behind. Gen. 19:17
Regretting; wasting time.

A pillar of salt. Gen. 19:26
Lifeless; stricken dead.

As the stars of heaven. Gen. 22:17
Many in number; a great multitude.

Went in at the gate. Gen. 23:18
Mature men who sat at the counsel.

Hand under thigh. Gen. 24:2
Hand under girdle; a solemn oath.

Tender eyed. Gen. 29:17
Attractive eyes.

He hath sold us. Gen. 31:15
He has devoured our dowry.

Wrestling with an angel. Gen. 32:24
Being suspicious of a pious man.

Coat of many colors. Gen. 37:23
A coat with long sleeves meaning learning, honor and a high position.

Spilling seed on the ground. Gen. 38:9
Spilling semen on the ground. (An ancient practice of birth control.)

No man shall lift up his hand or foot. Gen. 41:44
No man shall do anything without your approval.

Put his hand upon thine eyes. Gen. 46:4
Shall close your eyes upon your death bed.

Laying on of hands. Gen. 48:14
Blessing and approving a person.

His right hand upon the head. Gen. 48:17
A sincere blessing.

Unstable as water. Gen. 49:4
Undecided; in a dilemma.

The sceptre shall not depart from Judah. Gen. 49:10
There shall always be a king from the lineage of Judah.

Washed his garments in wine. Gen. 49:11
He will become an owner of many vineyards.

His teeth white with milk. Gen. 49:12
He will have abundant flocks of sheep.

His bow abode in strength. Gen. 49:24
He will become a valiant warrior.

The stone of Israel. Gen. 49:24
The strong race of Israel.

He gathered up his feet. Gen. 49:33
> *He stretched out his feet—He breathed his last breathe; he died.*

THE BOOK OF EXODUS

A burning bush. Ex. 3:2
> *Difficulties ahead.*

Not consumed. Ex. 3:2
> *Difficulties will be overcome; the task will be a success.*

Put off thy shoes. Ex. 3:5
> *Disregard pagan teachings. Cleanse your heart.*

Serpent. Ex. 4:3
> *An enemy; deception. Metaphorically—Pharaoh.*

Take it by the tail. Ex. 4:4
> *To overcome it, to defeat it. Truth triumphs over error.*

Hand in bosom. Ex. 4:6
> *To bring something new; a magical performance.*

He comes forth to the water. Ex. 8:20
> *He goes to the toilet.*

Behind the mill. Ex. 11:5
> *The poor, the ordinary and the blind who grind the grain.*

Pillar of fire. Ex. 13:21
> *Light at night; guidance.*

Pillar of cloud. Ex. 13:21
> *To lead and to protect from the heat of the day.*

The blast of thy nostrils. Ex. 15:8
> *Anger; displeasure.*

Manna. Ex. 16:15
> *What is it? (Aramaic)*

Smite the rock. Ex. 17:6
> *To discover the rock on the top of the hidden well. Searching for water in the desert. (See Old Testament Light.)*

Went up to God. Ex. 19:3
> *Went up to a high place.*

Eagles' wings. Ex. 19:4
> *Protection; speed; omnipresence.*

None shall appear before me empty. Ex. 23:15
> *No one shall appear before me empty handed, without a gift.*

Hornets. Ex. 23:28
> *Commandos or desert raiders; hit and run.*

They saw God. Ex. 24:11
> *Divine Presence felt.*

Written with the finger of God. Ex. 31:18
> *Perfect, flawless, without an error.*

They rose up to play. Ex. 32:6
> *They rose up to quarrel among themselves.*

Land flowing with milk and honey. Ex. 33:3
> *A fertile land; wisdom and spiritual understanding.*

A stiffnecked people. Ex. 33:3
> *A stubborn people.*

His face shone. Ex. 34:30
> *His face radiated; a spiritual manifestation.*

THE BOOK OF LEVITICUS

Covering of lips. Lev. 13:45
> *Keeping silent; caution against spreading of leprosy.*

Seed. Lev. 18:21
> *Offspring; semen; teaching.*

THE BOOK OF NUMBERS

Spirit of jealousy. Num. 5:14
An evil inclination which causes jealousy.

The fire of the Lord burned among them. Num. 11:1
Destruction, disaster, affliction.

Is the Lord's hand waxed short? Num. 11:23
Is the Lord unable to meet the needs of the people and to protect them?

While the flesh was yet between their teeth. Num. 11:33
They had plenty of food on hand and lacked nothing, but they were ungrateful.

Spitting in the face. Num. 12:14
A stern rebuke; a refutation of evil things.

They are bread for us. Num. 14:9
We can easily conquer them with little effort.

Another spirit with him. Num. 14:24
The true spiritual inclination.

Forty years. Num. 14:34
A holy number familiar to the people; a period of preparation, fasting and prayer.

Speak to the rock. Num. 20:8
Command the well to give its water. To discover the rock on the top of the well.

He smote the rock twice. Num. 20:11
Moses was doubtful. (God was angry because Moses did not strike once in trust and give the glory to God. See verse 12.)

The Lord opened the mouth of the ass. Num. 22:28
Balaam's stupidity; the stupid beast knew more than Balaam. (This incident took place in a vision.)

The dust of Jacob. Num. 23:10
The numerous descendants of Jacob.

A star out of Jacob. Num. 24:17
A bright future for the descendants of Jacob.

They shall be pricks in your eyes and thorns in your sides. Num.
33:55
*Your enemies will be a constant grievance and worry to you;
oppression and blunders.*

THE BOOK OF DEUTERONOMY

Face to face. Deut. 5:4
Openly, plainly, hiding nothing.

Not to turn aside to the right hand or to the left. Deut. 5:32
Not to deviate, keep the law.

God will send hornets. Deut. 7:20
God will send raiders, commandos, Arab bands.

Fenced up to heaven. Duet. 9:1
Well defended, fortified.

I (God) will write. Deut. 9:1
I (God) will dictate perfectly.

Circumcise the foreskin of your heart. Deut. 10:16
Purify your heart of all evil, rebellion and stubbornness.

Bind up the money in thine hand. Deut. 14:25
Guard your money, spend it carefully.

To be met with bread and water. Deut. 23:4
Friendly and sincere welcome.

Thou shalt have a place without the camp . . . thou shalt go forth
abroad. Deut. 23:12
You shall have a toilet outside the camp to relieve yourself.

Neither shall the sole of thy foot have rest. Deut. 28:65
You shall not have any land which you can call your own.

Trembling heart. Deut. 28:65
   Extreme fear.

Failing of eyes. Deut. 28:65
   No insight into the future.

Sorrow of mind. Deut. 28:65
   Regrets because of failure.

A root that beareth gall and wormwood. Deut. 29:18
   A corrupt person with evil deeds.

To add drunkenness to thirst. Deut. 29:19
   To add one evil to another.

Hide my face. Deut. 31:18
   Refuse to see you; turn away from you.

Doctrine drop as the rain. Deut. 32:2
   Truth from heaven, not by means of force or man's knowledge.

My speech shall distil as the dew. Deut. 32:2
   My speech shall be clearly and easily understood.

As the apple of his eye. Deut. 32:10
   He loved and took care of him as a man would care for his precious eyes.

Vine of Sodom. Deut. 32:32
   The Sodomite race; an evil people who practiced homosexuality.

Their wine is the poison of dragons, and the cruel venom of asps. Deut. 32:33
   Pagan teaching; corrupt practices and slanderous accusations.

Bullock and horns. Deut. 33:17
   Strength, honor and defense.

Let him dip his foot in oil. Deut. 33:24
   Let him become very prosperous. (Oil is symbolical of prosperity.)

Shoes shall be iron and brass. Deut. 33:25
   Inexhaustible supplies.

God who rideth upon the heaven. Deut. 33:26
> *Figuratively—a universal God. (Pagan gods rode on donkeys, mules and horses.)*

THE BOOK OF JOSHUA

To go out and to come in. Josh. 14:11
> *To lead the people out to war and to bring them in; leadership.*

THE BOOK OF JUDGES

A man left handed. Jud. 3:15
> *A good swordsman.*

White asses. Jud. 5:10
> *Symbol of dignity, purity and piety.*

Put your trust in my shadow. Jud. 9:15
> *Believe me and trust in my protection.*

God sent an evil spirit. Jud. 9:23
> *A grudge; an evil inclination.*

The Spirit of the Lord came upon him. Jud. 14:6
> *He prophesied.*

Plowed with my heifer. Jud. 14:18
> *Enticed my weak-minded wife.*

THE FIRST BOOK OF SAMUEL

Mine horn is exalted. 1 Sam. 2:1
> *My honor has been exalted.*

My mouth is enlarged. 1 Sam. 2:1
> *Now I can talk aloud and speak boldly.*

An evil spirit from the Lord troubled him. 1 Sam. 16:14
> *An evil inclination came upon him; the spirit of jealousy.*

He put his life in his hand. 1 Sam. 19:5
He exposed himself to danger.

He became as a stone. 1 Sam. 25:37
He was stricken, paralyzed.

THE SECOND BOOK OF SAMUEL

Dog's head. 2 Sam. 3:8
A leader of vicious men or bandits.

Except thou take away the blind and the lame. 2 Sam. 5:6
We will fight to the last man.

The kingdom. 2 Sam. 7:13
The term "kingdom" means "counsulship." "A king" means "a counselor."

As water split on the ground. 2 Sam. 14:14
We are perishable.

God of my rock. 2 Sam. 22:3
God of my strength and defense.

Smoke out of his nostrils. 2 Sam. 22:9
Very angry, enraged.

Fire out of his mouth. 2 Sam. 22:9
Strong denunciations.

He was seen upon the wings of the wind. 2 Sam. 22:11
He came very fast.

He drew out of many waters. 2 Sam. 22:17
He saved me out of many troubles.

He brought me forth into a large place. 2 Sam. 22:20
He relieved me from my distress.

Lamp. 2 Sam. 22:29
Light; understanding; an heir.

THE FIRST BOOK OF THE KINGS

And a chariot came up and went out of Egypt for six-hundred shekels of silver. 1 Kings 10:29
The price of chariots was up to six-hundred shekels.

Light (lamp). 1 Kings 11:36
An heir.

My little finger shall be thicker than my father's loins (thumb—Lamsa). 1 Kings 12:10
I am harsher than my father.

Pisseth against the wall. 1 Kings 14:10
Every mature person. (Mature men urinate against the wall not to be seen.)

Him that is shut up and left. 1 Kings 14:10
Anyone with authority.

The fire of the Lord. 1 Kings 18:38
Lightning.

Let not him that girdeth on his harness boast himself as he that putteth it off. 1 Kings 20:11
The one who ties a knot is not more able than the one who can untie it. (Lamsa)
He who destroys is stronger than he who builds.

THE SECOND BOOK OF THE KINGS

Chariot of fire and horses of fire. 2 Kings 2:11
Speed and a glorious manifestation.

Went up by a whirlwind into heaven. 2 Kings 2:11
A glorious departure from this life..

Bald head. 2 Kings 2:23
Metaphorically—a liar.

He leaneth on my hand. 2 Kings 5:18
I am his aide.

To give him always a light. 2 Kings 8:19
Give him an heir to sit on his throne.

Let us look one another in the face. 2 Kings 14:8
Let us face one another in battle.

There was not any shut up, not any left. 2 Kings 14:26
There was no man in power.

A bruised reed. 2 Kings 18:21
A weak ally.

The line of Samaria and the plummet of Ahab. 2 Kings 21:13
I will punish Jerusalem with the same measure of punishment like that of Samaria and the family of Ahab.

I will wipe Jerusalem as a man wipes a dish. 2 Kings 21:13
I will destroy Jerusalem completely.

THE FIRST BOOK OF THE CHRONICLES

The times that went over him. 1 Chron. 29:30
Periods of difficulty, trial and change.

THE SECOND BOOK OF THE CHRONICLES

The house was filled with a cloud. 2 Chron. 5:13
The temple was filled with the glory of God.

A light (lamp). 2 Chron. 21:7
An heir.

The Lord stirred up the spirit of Cyrus. 2 Chron. 36:22
The Lord prompted a desire or an inclination in Cyrus.

THE BOOK OF NEHEMIAH

If a fox go up, he shall break down their wall. Neh. 4:3
The wall was so weak that they had no defense.

THE BOOK OF JOB

Sons of God. Job. 1:6
Good men; believers in God.

Rent his mantle and shaved his head. Job. 1:20
Started to mourn.

Why is light given to a man whose way is hid? Job 3:23
Why is understanding or enlightenment given to a man who is unable to use it?

Feeble knees. Job 4:4
Weakness and uncertainty.

A spirit passed before my face. Job 4:15
I was in a vision.

In league with the stones of the field and the beast of the field. Job 5:23
Nature will be on your side.

Those who were afraid of ice, much snow has fallen upon them. Job 6:16
One who is afraid of a little trouble, receives much.

Spider's web. Job 8:14
Weakness; hopelessness.

Removeth the mountains. Job 9:5
To overcome insurmountable problems.

The hand of the Lord. Job 12:9
The Lord is aware of whatever happens.

I take my flesh in my teeth and my life in my hand. Job 13:14
I am so afflicted and my life is exposed to danger.

Born of a woman. Job 14:1
Weak; human being; subject to temptation.

Fill his belly with the East wind. Job 15:2
Proud, bragging, boasting.

Defiled my horn in the dust. Job 16:15
Humbled my honor.

His candle shall be put out. Job 18:6
His heir shall die.

He hath swallowed down riches and he shall vomit them up
again. Job 20:15
He has acquired riches by embezzlement and shall lose them.

God shall cast them out of His belly. Job 20:15
God will destroy them.

Brooks of honey and butter. Job 20:17
Prosperity; God's abundance.

With the measure with which he had measured, he shall be
recompensed. (Lamsa) Job 20:22
The law of compensation.

Arms of the fatherless have been broken. Job 22:9
Orphans left helpless; harassed.

They have inherited a ruined mine. (Lamsa) Job 28:4
They have inherited a defective heritage.

His candle. Job 29:3
God's light and His truth shining.

When I washed my steps with butter. Job 29:6
When I was very wealthy.

Laid their hand on their mouth. Job 29:9
They were speechless.

I was eyes to the blind. Job 29:15
I gave good counsel to the unlearned.

I was feet to the lame. Job 29:15
I was help to the helpless.

Then I said, I shall be straight like a reed. (Lamsa) Job 29:18
Then I said, I shall be honest and straight forward.

I am a brother to dragons, and a companion to owls. Job 30:29
I have become an outcast living in desolate places.

Then let my wife grind for another and let her bake bread at another man's place. (Lamsa) Job 31:10
Let me become destitute.

To have caused the eyes of the widow to fail. Job 31:16
To have defrauded the widow or taken advantage of her.

My mouth hath kissed my hand. Job 31:27
Taking a high profit or cheating in business.

My belly is as wine which hath no vent. Job 32:19
I cannot keep the secret any longer.

The stars sang. Job 38:7
The universe sharing in man's joy; harmony.

THE BOOK OF PSALMS

Kiss the Son. Ps. 2:12
To do obeisance; to obey him.

I water my bed and wash my mattress with tears. Ps. 6:6
I weep bitterly.

Sucklings. Ps. 8:2
Little children; unlearned men.

Son of man. Ps. 8:4
Mankind; a human being.

Lift up thine hand. Ps. 10:12
Take action; fight.

Double heart. Ps. 12:2
Two-faced; insincere; doubtful.

Cut off all flattering lips. Ps. 12:3
Shut up, be quiet.

Eat up my people. Ps. 14:4
    Devour my people; oppress, exploit.

Cup of goodness. Ps. 16:5
    Good fortune.

The shadow of thy wings. Ps. 17:8
    Your protection.

Rock. Ps. 18:2
    Protection and defense.

The floods. Ps. 18:4
    Troubles; invasions.

He made darkness his secret place. Ps. 18:11
    He is hidden from human eyes.

Thou wilt light my candle. Ps. 18:28
    He will give me light and happiness. He will give me an heir.

Dogs. Ps. 22:16
    Vicious men; gossipers.

Seed. Ps. 22:30
    Posterity.

Wash my hands in innocency. Ps. 26:6
    Absolved from guilt.

My foot standeth in an even place. Ps. 26:12
    I am steady and shall stand firm.

The Lord sitteth upon the flood. Ps. 29:10
    God is in control. He crushes the armies of the enemy.

Sons of men. Ps. 31:19
    Worldly men.

Lions. Ps. 35:17
    Dictators; oppressors.

Wink with the eye. Ps. 35:19
    Insincere, deceptive.

Fatness of thy house. Ps. 36:8
Abundant joys; prosperity of your house.

My tears have been my meat (bread) day and night. Ps. 42:3
I cried even while eating. I am harassed.

There is a river. Ps. 46:4
There is an eternal truth.

They graze like cattle. (Lamsa) Ps. 49:13
They are demented; insane.

Create in me a clean heart. Ps. 51:10
Make me to be born again; put out the error in exchange for the truth.

Renew a right spirit within me. Ps. 51:10
Grant me right thinking, right inclinations.

Scattered their bones. Ps. 53:5
Destroyed them; broke their power.

Poison of a serpent. Ps. 58:4
Wrong teaching; slanderous remarks.

As a snail (as wax—Lamsa) which melteth. Ps. 58:8
To pass away; to be destroyed.

Thorns. Ps. 58:9
Difficulties; annoyances; grievances.

Make a noise like a dog. Ps. 59:14
Threaten to talk and do nothing.

Moab is my wash pot. Ps. 60:8
Moab is nothing. He is my servant.

Lead me to the rock. Ps. 61:2
Lead me to the protection of God.

That thy way may be known. Ps. 67:2
That God's religion may be known.

Ye have lien among the pots. Ps. 68:13
Though you sleep among the thorns. (Lamsa)
> *Living in difficulties.*

Hills leap. Ps. 68:16
> *People rejoicing; period of prosperity.*

The depths of the sea. Ps. 68:22
> *Utter hopelessness.*

Thy foot dipped in the blood. Ps. 68:23
> *A great slaughter.*

Fountain of Israel. Ps. 68:26
> *Religion, truth of Israel.*

The zeal of thy house hath eaten me up. Ps. 69:9
> *The zeal of thy house has made me courageous, has provoked me*
> *to act.*

Table as a snare. Ps. 69:22
> *Meeting for a conspiracy that would lead to failure.*

Dragon. Ps. 74:13
> *A great dictator.*

Wine and dregs. Ps. 75:8
> *Wine mixed with poison; corrupt teachings.*

Thy way is in the sea. Ps. 77:19
> *Your way leaves no imprints. It is hidden from the eyes of the flesh.*

Bread of tears. Ps. 80:5
> *Oppression; persecution; poverty.*

Vine out of Egypt. Ps. 80:8
> *Israel out of Egypt.*

The boar. Ps. 80:13
> *The enemies of Israel.*

Selah. Ps. 84:8
> *Attention, ready. A war song.*

His hand in the sea and his right hand in the rivers. Ps. 89:25
He shall have dominion over the islands in the sea and the lands of the river, namely Egypt and Assyria.

Shadow. Ps. 91:1
Protection.

Snare of the fowler. Ps. 91:3
Evil devices.

God's feathers. Ps. 91:4
God's tender mercies.

Pestilence that walks in darkness. Ps. 91:6
Conspiracy that spreads during the darkness.

Viper and adder. (Lamsa) Ps. 91:13
Deadly enemies; evil forces.

Lion. (Lamsa) Ps. 91:13
Imperial power.

My days are consumed like smoke. Ps. 102:3
My days are wasting away; fleeting.

I have eaten ashes like bread. Ps. 102:9
I have suffered hunger and privation.

He openeth the rock. Ps. 105:41
He found the well; he bore the rock.

My heart is fixed. Ps. 108:1
I am ready.

Satan stands at his right hand. Ps. 109:6
He receives wrong counsel.

Sit at my right hand. Ps. 110:1
I will trust you and grant you power.

The stone which the builder rejected. Ps. 118:22
A good leader rejected.

My hands also will I lift up unto thy commandments. Ps. 119:48
I will take an oath with your commandments.

I am become like a bottle in the smoke. Ps. 119:83
I have become like a frozen sheepskin. (Lamsa)
I have suffered all disgrace. I was harassed.

A lamp unto my feet. Ps. 119:105
Guidance; a light unto man's feet.

Rivers of waters run down mine eyes. Ps. 119:36
I wept bitterly.

Look to the hand. Ps. 123:2
Depend on; to wait upon.

Sow in tears. Ps. 126:5
Shortage of food in the Spring. (The sower weeps when he scatters his precious seed in the ground while his children are hungry.)

Reap in joy. Ps. 126:5
The famine is over and food is abundant.

My downsitting and uprising. Ps. 139:2
My conduct; my affairs.

Corner stones. Ps. 144:12
Beautiful in character; chaste.

Son of man. Ps. 146:3
An ordinary man; a human being.

THE BOOK OF PROVERBS

Pour out my spirit unto you. Prov. 1:23
Give you power and understanding.

They shall eat of the fruit of their own way. Prov. 1:31
They shall suffer for their own evil deeds.

Buckler. Prov. 2:7
Protection and defense.

Bind them about thy neck. Prov. 3:3
> *Be mindful of them and do not forget them.*

Grace to your neck. Prov. 3:22
> *You will receive honor, glory and grace.*

Drink the wine of violence. Prov. 4:17
> *Rage, extortion and other evil things.*

Let thine eyes look right on. Prov. 4:25
> *Be honest and sincere.*

Drink waters out of thine own cistern, and running waters out
of thine own well. Prov. 5:15
> *Love your own wife and keep away from other women.*

Rivers of waters in the street. Prov. 5:16
> *Many children in the streets.*

Let thy fountain be blessed. Prov. 5:18
> *Let thy virility be blessed.*

Bind them upon thy fingers. Prov. 7:3
> *Be constantly mindful of them.*

Stolen waters. Prov. 9:17
> *Stolen love.*

Bread eaten in secret is pleasant. Prov. 9:17
> *Making love to another woman in secret appears pleasant.*

The tree of life. Prov. 11:30
> *A good family.*

He that keepeth his mouth keepeth his life. Prov. 13:3
> *He who talks less keeps out of trouble and spares his life.*

A wounded spirit. Prov. 18:14
> *Hurt pride.*

Hasty feet. Prov. 19:2
> *Ready to do evil and commit crimes.*

Mouth filled with gravel. Prov. 20:17
> *Cannot give an answer or exonerate himself for his evil deed.*

Knife in your throat. Prov. 23:2
> *To be poisoned.*

Swallows pitch. (Lamsa) Prov. 23:7
> *A superb liar.*

Vomit up. Prov. 23:8
> *You shall pay for it; the law of compensation.*

Red eyes. Prov. 23:29
> *Drunkenness.*

Lieth down in the midst of the sea. Prov. 23:34
> *Lost; in a dilemma; senseless; in doubt.*

Lieth upon the top of the mast. Prov. 23:34
A sailor in a tempest. (Lamsa)
> *In confusion; doubtful; undecided.*

Wisdom is too high for a fool; he openeth not his mouth in the gate. Prov. 24:7
> *He cannot give counsel at the gate. (In the East, meetings are held at the town gate.)*

Dropping of sand on the string of a musical instrument. (Lamsa) Prov. 25:20
> *Wasting time.*

Heap coals of fire upon his head. Prov. 25:22
> *Do good to him so that you may cause him to regret the evil he has done to you.*

Thorn in the hand of a drunkard. Prov. 26:9
> *A drunkard's difficulties and grievances multiply.*

A dog returneth to his vomit. Prov. 26:11
> *A man who repeats his mistakes.*

One that takes a dog by the ears. Prov. 26:17
> *One who meddles with a situation and does not know how to handle it.*

Hides his hand in his bosom. Prov. 26:15
> *Too lazy to work; idleness.*

It grieves him to bring it again to his mouth. Prov. 26:15
> *He is extremely lazy and even eating is considered a heavy task.*

Known in the gate. Prov. 31:23
> *Outstanding person in the counsel; well known in town.*

ECCLESIASTES

I praise the dead more than the living. Eccles. 4:2
> *The dead are at peace but the living continue to struggle in order to live.*

A wise man's heart is at his right hand; but a fool's heart at his left. Eccles. 10:2
> *A wise man renders a good decision but a fool does not know how to render a good decision.*

He that digs a pit shall fall into it. Eccles. 10:8
> *He who tries to devise evil against his neighbor shall fall into it himself.*

He knoweth not how to go to the city. Eccles. 10:15
> *He does not know how to buy and sell.*

Cast thy bread upon the water and thou shalt find it. Eccles. 11:1
> *Give charity and you will get it back.*

While the sun, or the light, or the moon, or the stars, be not darkened. Eccles. 12:2
> *Before life ebbs, beauty fades, fortune fails.*

Nor the clouds return after the rain. Eccles. 12:2
> *Poverty returns after prosperity.*

Keepers of the house shall tremble. Eccles. 12:3
Legs shall weaken.

The strong men shall bow themselves. Eccles. 12:3
Arms shall become weak.

The grinders cease because they are few. Eccles. 12:3
The teeth chew no more because they are few.

Those that look out of the windows be darkened. Eccles. 12:3
The eyes are dimmed.

The doors shall be shut in the streets, when the sound of the grinding is low. Eccles. 12:4
The ears shall be so dulled that the sound of women grinding at the mill is low.

He shall rise up at the voice of the bird. Eccles. 12:4
The man is so old that even the sound of a bird will keep him awake.

The almond tree shall flourish. Eccles. 12:4
His children shall be multiplied speedily. (An almond tree blossoms all at once and is symbolic of speed.)

The grasshopper shall be a burden. Eccles. 12:5
The locust shall be multiplied. (Lamsa)
Man shall see his children, grandchildren and great grandchildren.

Silver cord be loosed. (cut off—Lamsa) Eccles. 12:6
Physical desire fades away.

The golden bowl be broken. Eccles. 12:6
Life comes to an end.

The pitcher be broken at the fountain. Eccles. 12:6
Virility stops and life comes to an end.

The wheel broken at the cistern. Eccles. 12:6
Impotent.

The words of the wise are as goads and as nails. Eccles. 12:11
The words of the wise make deep and lasting impressions.

THE SONG OF SOLOMON

Honey and milk are under thy tongue. Song of Sol. 4:11
Sweet speech and wisdom.

A garden inclosed is my sister, my spouse. Song of Sol. 4:12
Metaphorically—a very beloved wife.

Set me as a seal upon thine heart and arm. Song of Sol. 8:6
Keep me in your mind and love me with your strength.

Love is as strong as death. Song of Sol. 8:6
Death snatches life away and love conquers man's heart and desire.

Desire is cruel as Sheol. (Lamsa) Song of Sol. 8:6
Desire is hard to be conquered.

Many waters cannot quench love. Song of Sol. 8:7
Love is supreme and unconquerable.

She hath no breast. Song of Sol. 8:8
She is not mature.

THE BOOK OF THE PROPHET ISAIAH

A cottage in the vineyard. Isa. 1:8
Deserted and desolate. (The cottage is deserted after the gathering of the grapes.)

Everyone loveth gifts. Isa. 1:23
Everyone loves bribes.

Mountain. Isa. 2:2
Metaphorically—Israel. "Mountain" also means "a problem."

Enter into the rock, and hide in the dust. Isa. 2:10
Take refuge in a cave; flee for your life.

Cedars of Lebanon. Isa. 2:13
> *Great and noble men.*

Breath in his nostrils. Isa. 2:22
> *Hasty, impulsive, impatient and angry.*

Take away the stay and the staff. Isa. 3:1
> *Take away all substance, supply and blessings.*

Vineyard of God. Isa. 5:1
> *Metaphorically—Israel.*

Unclean lips. Isa. 6:5
> *Sinful, unworthy.*

Smoking firebrands. Isa. 7:4
> *Trouble makers.*

Virgin. Isa. 7:14
> *Purity and chastity.*

Butter and honey. Isa. 7:15
> *Wisdom, harmony, prosperity.*

The Lord shall hiss (whistle—Lamsa). Isa. 7:18
> *The Lord shall summon.*

Flies and bees. Isa. 7:18
> *Large armies of the Assyrians and Egyptians.*

I went unto the prophetess. Isa. 8:3
> *I had intercourse with the prophetess. (This incident took place in a vision.) A treaty with Assyria.*

A rod out of the stem of Jesse. Isa. 11:1
> *An heir from the family of Jesse.*

The rod of his mouth. Isa. 11:4
> *Strong and true words.*

The breath of his lips. Isa. 11:4
> *His commands, his stern utterances.*

Girdle of his loins. Isa. 11:5
Strength, authority and readiness.

The wolf and the lamb shall dwell together. Isa. 11:6
An oppressor and a weak nation shall live together in peace.

The leopard shall lie down with the kid. Isa. 11:6
A dictator and a helpless nation shall be at peace.

A little child shall lead them. Isa. 11:6
An unlearned man shall be able to govern them.

The cow and the bear shall feed. Isa. 11:7
The powerful and small nations shall trade together and live in harmony.

The lion shall eat straw like an ox. Isa. 11:7
Powerful nations shall be satisfied with what they have. They will not devour small nations.

The suckling child shall play on the hole of the asp. Isa 11:8
A small nation shall not be afraid of a powerful nation.

The weaned child shall put his hand on the cockatrice den. Isa. 11:8
A small nation shall be able to handle their deadly enemies.

They shall not hurt nor destroy in all my holy mountain. Isa. 11:9
They shall not plunder nor oppress Israel.

A root of Jesse. Isa. 11:10
Posterity of Jesse. True teaching of Judaism.

A highway for the remnant. Isa. 11:16
Understanding between the Jews and the great imperial powers of Assyria and Egypt.

Water of salvation. Isa. 12:3
Truth and spiritual understanding flowing out of Judaism.

A branch. Isa. 14:19
A rejected heir. (The house of David was rejected.)

A smoke from the north. Isa. 14:31
A disaster from the north; an invasion.

My bowels shall sound like an harp. Isa. 16:11
My heart shall lament.

Neither shall there be any work for Egypt, which the head or tail, branch or rush, may do. Isa. 19:15
There shall be no leader in Egypt who can govern.

Highway out of Egypt to Assyria. Isa. 19:23
An understanding between Egypt and Assyria.

The key of the house of David. Isa. 22:22
The authority and power of the house of David.

He shall open and none shall shut. Isa. 22:22
Total authority.

We have been with child; we have as it were brought forth wind. Isa. 26:18
We have been expecting good but we have received nothing.

A vineyard of red wine. Isa. 27:2
A life-giving religion; true Judaism.

Briers and thorns. Isa. 27:4
Difficulties and grievances.

Fat valley. Isa. 28:1
Fertile valley.

Drunkard of Ephraim. Isa. 28:1
Drunken with power and not with wine.

The spirit of deep sleep. Isa. 29:10
An inclination of dullness.

Shadow of Egypt. Isa. 30:2
An alliance with Egypt; protection under Egypt.

The light of the moon shall be as the light of the sun, and the light of the sun shall be sevenfold. Isa. 30:26
> *Knowledge and truth shall be multiplied. (The sun is symbolical of God, and the moon is symbolical of the earth or man.)*

The sword shall be bathed in heaven. Isa. 34:5
> *God's mighty power.*

The sword of the Lord is filled with blood. Isa. 34:6
> *Impending slaughter; vengeance.*

The staff of the broken reed. Isa. 36:6
> *A weak ally, namely Egypt.*

Shepherd's tent. Isa. 38:12
> *Temporal life.*

Weaver's web. (Lamsa) Isa. 38:12
> *Short span of life.*

Crooked made straight. Isa. 40:4
> *Injustices corrected.*

Valleys exalted. Isa. 40:4
> *The meek exalted.*

Mountains made low. Isa. 40:4
> *Proud nations humbled.*

All flesh is grass. Isa. 40:6
> *Man's earthly life is temporal like grass.*

Threshing instrument having teeth. Isa. 41:15
> *A powerful and ruthless nation.*

Make the hills as chaff. Isa. 41:15
> *Destroy small and aggressive nations.*

Thresh the mountains and beat them small. Isa. 41:15
> *To conquer imperial powers and reduce them to small kingdoms.*

Wilderness and the cities lift up their voice. Isa. 42:11
> *Let the helpless nations rejoice and receive enlightenment.*

Let the inhabitants of the rock sing. Isa. 42:11
> *Let the inhabitants of Petra (rock) sing. (Petra was the capital of Edom.)*

Make a way in the wilderness. Isa. 43:19
> *Bring understanding among the desert people, the illiterate people.*

Rivers in the desert. Isa. 43:19
> *Knowledge and understanding among the desert people.*

The beast of the field shall honor me. Isa. 43:20
> *Savage tribes shall honor me.*

The dragons and the owls. Isa. 43:20
> *Wild desert chiefs shall honor me.*

Because I give waters in the wilderness and rivers in the desert. Isa. 43:20
> *Because I give knowledge and truth to the desert people, the illiterate people.*

Calling a ravenous bird. Isa. 46:11
> *Calling a dictator who takes swift action and devours.*

Called me from the womb. Isa. 49:1
> *I was ordained when I was conceived.*

I have graven thee upon the palms of my hands. Isa. 49:16
> *I will remember you continually.*

Eat their own flesh. (Lamsa) Isa. 49:26
> *Endure hardships. Facing a siege.*

All ye that kindle a fire. Isa. 50:11
All of you are like kindling wood. (Lamsa)
> *All of you are worthless and responsible for disasters.*

Wild bull in the net. Isa. 51:20
They are faded like a wilted beet. (Lamsa)
> *They are humiliated and crushed.*

Drunk but not with wine. Isa. 51:21
> *Drunk with power and evil doings.*

Shake thyself from the dust. Isa. 52:2
> *Free yourself and start to act. Stop mourning.*

Feet of good tidings. Isa. 52:7
> *Men who bring good news.*

Sprinkle many nations. Isa. 52:15
> *To purify many nations.*

The arm of the Lord revealed. Isa. 53:1
> *The strength and power of the Lord revealed.*

A tender plant. Isa. 53:2
An infant. (Lamsa)
> *Pure, simple and sincere.*

A root out of a dry ground. Isa. 53:2
> *An heir from an extinct family. (The house of David.)*

He hath no form nor comeliness. Isa. 53:2
> *He has not the character of a strong leader.*

Smitten of God. Isa. 53:4
> *A severe punishment like that inflicted upon Job.*

As a sheep before her shearers. Isa. 53:7
> *Gentle, not protesting.*

Prosper in his hand. Isa. 53:10
> *He will be blessed and have command. He will have control.*

Blind watchmen. Isa. 56:10
> *False prophets; short-sighted leaders.*

Dumb dogs that cannot bark. Isa. 65:10
> *Vicious and indifferent leaders.*

The Lord's hand is not shortened. Isa. 59:1
> *The Lord is not weak nor is he unable to do.*

Thy light is come. Isa. 60:1
> *Your truth has been revealed.*

Darkness. Isa. 60:2
Ignorance and disaster.

Suck the milk of the Gentiles. Isa. 60:16
To acquire the wealth of foreign nations.

Thou shalt suck the breast of kings. Isa. 60:16
You shall drain the wealth of kings.

Garments of salvation. Isa. 61:10
Good and righteous deeds.

As a lamp that burns. Isa. 62:1
An everlasting Salvation.

Red in thine apparel, and garments like him that tread in the
winefat. Isa. 63:2
Severe punishment and bloodshed.

Make them drunk in my fury. Isa. 63:6
Make them confused and ready to suffer.

The sounding of the bowels. Isa. 63:15
Your tender mercies.

New heavens and a new earth. Isa. 65:17
A new world order with true justice and peace.

The wolf and the lamb feed together. Isa. 65:25
*A dictatorship and a meek nation trading and living together in
peace.*

Dust shall be the serpent's meat. Isa. 65:25
The oppressor shall be reduced to poverty; humbled.

Ye may suck. Isa. 66:11
You shall become rich and well nourished.

THE BOOK OF THE PROPHET JEREMIAH

I am a child. Jer. 1:6
I am unlearned, inexperienced.

Almond tree. Jer. 1:11
A hasty occurrence; speed. (The almond tree blossoms all at once.)

Seething pot. Jer. 1:13
Disaster is brewing.

Shadow of death. Jer. 2:6
Sudden danger, death.

Pastors. Jer. 2:8
Rulers and leaders.

Fountain of living waters. Jer. 2:13
The truth; true Jewish religion.

Wild ass. Jer. 2:24
Out of control.

A whore's forehead. Jer. 3:3
A shameless woman; daring to do evil.

Played the harlot. Jer. 3:6
Worshipped other gods.

Become wind. Jer. 5:13
Without a message.

Watchmen. Jer. 6:17
Prophets.

The pen of the scribes is in vain. Jer. 8:8
Scribes forged some of the passages in the Scriptures.

I am black. Jer. 8:21
I am ashamed; I am sorrowful.

Wormwood. Jer. 9:15
Bitterness.

Water of gall. Jer. 9:15
Bitterness and distress.

Eaten up Jacob. Jer. 10:25
They have oppressed and devoured Jacob (Israel).

I discover thy skirts upon thy face. Jer. 13:26
I will cause your skirts to be uncovered and lifted over your face.
(Lamsa)
> *Shame and utter defeat.*

Sin written with a pen of iron. Jer. 17:1
> *Written clearly; evident, very obvious.*

Maketh flesh his arm. Jer. 17:5
> *Trusting in human power and human wisdom.*

Written in the earth. Jer. 17:13
> *Obliterated, forgotten.*

The burden of the Lord. Jer. 23:33
> *A message, a prophesy from the Lord.*

Baskets of figs. Jer. 24:1
> *Symbolical of people.*

Good figs. Jer. 24:3
> *Good people.*

Evil figs. Jer. 24:3
> *Evil people.*

Take the cup. Jer. 25:28
> *Take the punishment which is due; severe defeat.*

Lover. Jer. 30:14
> *An ally.*

Bullock. Jer. 31:18
> *Hard to subdue and train.*

I will sow. Jer. 31:27
> *I will repopulate, replenish.*

Written on the heart. Jer. 31:33
> *Written in the mind never to be forgotten.*

One heart. Jer. 32:39
> *One mind, one accord.*

As a shepherd putteth on his garment. Jer. 43:12
>   *Conquered very easily.*

Lost sheep. Jer. 50:6
>   *Lost people.*

Given her hand. Jer. 50:15
>   *Surrendering unconditionally.*

They shall become as women. Jer. 50:37
>   *They shall become cowards.*

A destroying mountain. Jer. 51:25
>   *A great potentate.*

The sea is come up upon Babylon. Jer. 51:42
>   *Babylon is overwhelmed.*

THE LAMENTATIONS OF JEREMIAH

Among all her lovers. Lam. 1:2
>   *Among all the Kings who had made a league with her.*

Virgins are afflicted. Lam. 1:4
>   *The virgins are raped.*

I called for my lovers. Lam. 1:19
>   *I called for my allies.*

Hath swallowed up. Lam. 2:2
>   *Drowned; devoured; completely destroyed.*

Cut off the horn. Lam. 2:3
>   *Destroyed the strength and honor of Judah.*

My liver is poured upon the earth. Lam. 2:11
>   *My pride is low to the ground.*

Tears run down like a river. Lam. 2:18
>   *I wept bitterly.*

Bear (wolf—Lamsa). Lam. 3:10
>   *A great destroyer.*

He putteth his mouth in the dust. Lam. 3:29
He is greatly humiliated.

He giveth his cheek to him that smiteth him. Lam. 3:30
He does not resist evil.

My eye runneth down with rivers of water. Lam. 3:48
I am weeping bitterly.

Waters flowed over mine head. Lam. 3:54
I was surrounded with many difficulties. I was in a dilemma.

I am their music. Lam. 3:63
They gossip about me.

We have given the hand. Lam. 5:6
We have surrendered to our enemies unconditionally.

Our fathers sinned and are not. Lam. 5:7
Our fathers sinned and died.

Our skin was black like an oven. Lam. 5:10
Ashamed and harassed.

THE BOOK OF THE PROPHET EZEKIEL

The face of a man. Ezk. 1:10
Intellect.

The face of a lion. Ezk. 1:10
Dominion.

The face of an ox. Ezk. 1:10
Strength, endurance.

The face of an eagle. Ezk. 1:10
Omnipresence.

Their rings (rims—Lamsa) were full of eyes. Ezk. 1:18
Eyes are symbolical of intelligence, strategy.

When the living creatures were lifted up from the earth, the wheels were lifted with them. Ezk. 1:19
> *When the cavalry went forward the infantry followed.*

Son of Man. Ezk. 2:1
> *A human being; an ordinary man.*

The book written within and without. Ezk. 2:10
> *The book containing past, present and future. The good and bad deeds of their fore-fathers.*

Eat the roll. Ezk. 3:1
> *Study it, analyze it and make it a part of you.*

Sweetness in my mouth. Ezk. 3:3
> *Sweetness in this instance means bitterness and sorrow.*

The spirit took me up. Ezk. 3:12
> *I was carried away in a vision.*

Noise of the wings. Ezk. 3:13
> *Symbolical of cavalry, speed. (Chaldean horsemen.)*

The noise of wheel. Ezk. 3:13
> *Symbolical of the speed of an infantry.*

The spirit lifted me up. Ezk. 3:14
> *I was prophesying.*

The hand of the Lord was upon me. Ezk. 3:22
> *I was in a vision.*

The spirit entered into me. Ezk. 3:24
> *I was inspired.*

I will make thy tongue cleave to the roof of thy mouth. Ezk. 3:26
> *I will make you speechless, stunned.*

Bake barley cakes with dung. Ezk. 4:12
> *Long siege; severe famine.*

Set thy face toward the mountains of Israel. Ezk. 6:2
> *Prophesy about Israel.*

Smite with thine hand, and stamp with thy foot. Ezk. 6:11
> *A sign of regret and astonishment.*

Brightness. Ezk. 8:2
> *God's presence.*

Image of jealousy (lust—Lamsa). Ezk. 8:3
> *A naked statue of a woman.*

Girdles of sapphire. (Lamsa) Ezk. 9:2
> *Authority, royalty.*

Spirit of the Lord fell upon me. Ezk. 11:5
> *I was in a vision.*

Stony heart. Ezk. 11:19
> *Stubborn.*

Follow their own spirit. Ezk. 13:3
> *Follow their own pride; wrong inclinations.*

Untempered mortar. Ezk. 13:15
> *Symbolical of weak alliances.*

Noisome beasts. Ezk. 14:15
> *Vicious men, evil men.*

Great of flesh. Ezk. 16:26
> *Men of large sex organs.*

Gifts to all whores. Ezk. 16:33
> *Payment for the harlots.*

Highest branch of the cedar. Ezk. 17:3
> *The royal family; the heirs of Judah.*

A great eagle. Ezk. 17:3
> *A swift conqueror.*

Under it shall dwell all fowl of every wing. Ezk. 17:23
> *All people shall embrace the true religion of Israel.*

That hath not eaten upon the mountain. Ezk. 18:15
> *That hath not worshipped false gods in high places.*

Lioness. Ezk. 19:2
> *Symbolical of the queen of Judah. The mother of the King.*

Lifted up my hand. Ezk. 20:5
> *Made a promise; taken an oath.*

Green tree. Ezk. 20:47
> *An innocent man.*

Dry tree. Ezk. 20:47
> *An evil man.*

They eat upon the mountains. Ezk. 22:9
> *They worship Baal.*

I have smitten my hands. Ezk. 22:13
> *I was shocked.*

Whose flesh is as the flesh of asses and horses. Ezk. 23:20
> *Whose male organs are like those of asses and horses.*

Thou shalt drink of thy sister's cup. Ezk. 23:32
> *You (Judah) will suffer the same punishment as your sister (Israel).*

Cover not thy lips. Ezk. 24:17
> *Do not mourn.*

All the princes of the sea. Ezk. 26:16
> *Princes of the islands, naval powers.*

No more a pricking brier. Ezk. 28:24
> *No more annoyances and enemies.*

Opening of the mouth. Ezk. 29:21
> *Boldness, talking back.*

Cloudy day. Ezk. 30:3
> *An evil day. An uncertain day.*

The day darkened and a cloud shall cover. Ezk. 30:18
Impending disaster and sorrow.

Assyrian a cedar. Ezk. 31:3
A great and tall people.

Fill your valleys with your dust. (Lamsa) Ezk. 32:5
I will inflict a heavy slaughter upon your army.

Raise up a plant. Ezk. 34:29
A new generation.

Can these bones live? Ezk. 37:3
Can crushed Israel rise again?

I will open your graves and cause you to come out. Ezk. 37:12
I will start you again as a new nation.

City without walls. Ezk. 38:11
City without enemies and thieves, without defenses.

Every feathered fowl, and beast of the field. Ezk. 39:17
A great slaughter. An impending disaster.

Hiding the face. Ezk. 39:23
Refusing to see anyone, ashamed.

Upon a very high mountain. Ezk. 40:2
High in consciousness.

Circumcise your heart. Ezk. 44:7
Be sincere in your heart and mind.

Water from the foundation of the house. Ezk. 47:1
Eternal truth, indestructible.

Healing waters. Ezk. 47:9
Truth; conversion.

Tree of righteousness.
Good men established by the Lord.

THE BOOK OF DANIEL

Changeth the times. Dan. 2:21
Good times and bad times; rise and fall of kingdoms.

Stone cut out without hand. Dan. 2:34
A true religion; truth not devised by men.

Eat grass as an ox. Dan. 4:32
To lose your mind, to be demented.

An excellent spirit. Dan. 6:3
Truthful, honest, sincere.

The four great beasts. Dan. 7:3
Four great imperial powers.

The first beast. Dan. 7:4
The Chaldean empire.

The second beast. Dan. 7:5
The Persian empire.

The third beast. Dan. 7:6
The Grecian empire.

The fourth beast. Dan. 7:7
The Roman empire.

The Ancient of days. Dan. 7:9
The Messiah.

Books opened. Dan. 7:10
The law of God made manifest; secrets and prophecies revealed.

Came with the clouds of glory. Dan. 7:13
Came with great honor and glory.

Teeth of iron. Dan. 7:19
Savage, vicious and devouring.

Nails of brass. Dan. 7:19
Strong.

Ram. Dan. 8:3
Persian empire.

He goat. Dan. 8:5
Grecian empire. Alexander the Great.

A little horn. Dan. 8:9
A small kingdom.

His face as the appearance of lightning. Dan. 10:6
Brilliancy, awe and frightening.

HOSEA

Hedge up thy way with thorns. Hos. 2:6
Make your way difficult; to restrain.

Lovers. Hos. 2:10
False allies.

I will sow her. Hos. 2:23
I will cause her to multiply.

They eat up the sin of my people. Hos. 4:8
They oppress my people, treat them wrongly.

Wind hath bound her up. Hos. 4:19
Carried away by her own evil devices, her own pride.

As an oven heated by the baker. Hos. 7:4
A strong passion.

A deceitful bow. Hos. 7:16
They miss the mark; to go astray.

Thorns in their tabernacles (tents). Hos. 9:6
Their tents deserted; without habitation.

Feedeth on wind. Hos. 12:1
Crazy; demented.

Followeth after the east wind. Hos. 12:1
Deceived, strongly misled.

I will ransom them from the grave and redeem them from death.
Hos. 13:14
I will restore them and get them out of their difficulties.

JOEL

All faces shall gather blackness. Joel 2:6
All faces shall be ashamed, confounded.

Winepresses shall overflow with wine and oil. (Lamsa) Joel
2:24
A bright and happy future.

Hills shall flow with milk. Joel 3:18
A period of peace and prosperity.

Mountains drop down new wine. Joel 3:18
New teaching and renewed joy.

A fountain shall come forth of the house of the Lord. Joel
3:18
Light of the truth; reformed Judaism.

AMOS

Kine of Bashan. Amos 4:1
Oppressors and dictators of Bashan.

Who turneth the shadow of death into the morning. Amos 5:8
Who changes an impending disaster into happiness.

Drink wine in bowls. Amos 6:6
Drunkards, addicts to wine.

OBADIAH

Return upon your own head. Obad. 1:15
You will pay for it.

JONAH

The word of the Lord came unto Jonah. Jonah 1:1
Jonah was in a vision.

Out of the belly of hell cried I. Jonah 2:2
While I was in difficulties and a dilemma I cried out for help.

Cast into the midst of the seas. Jonah 2:3
Lost; in great difficulty.

I went down to the bottoms of the mountains. Jonah 2:6
I was cut off from this world.

MICAH

I will make Samaria as an heap of the field (as a ploughed field
—Lamsa). Mic. 1:6
I will utterly destroy it.

Walks in the spirit of falsehood. Mic. 2:11
A deceitful inclination; prophesying falsely.

Eat the flesh of my people. Mic. 3:3
Devour and oppress my people.

Mountain of the Lord. Mic. 4:1
The Kingdom of the Lord. (Israel.)

As a dew from the Lord, as the showers upon the grass. Mic. 5:7
As a blessing from the Lord.

Rivers of oil. Mic. 6:7
Abundant wealth, prosperity.

Rags eaten by the moth. (Lamsa) Mic. 7:4
Good for nothing, rejected.

NAHUM

Your people are as women. Nah. 3:13
Your people are cowards.

HABAKKUK

Stone cry out. Hab. 2:11
Even nature will protest unrighteousness.

Displeased against the rivers. Hab. 3:8
Displeased against the great imperial powers of Babylon and Egypt. (Euphrates and Nile.)

Mountains trembled. Hab. 3:10
Great nations trembled.

The sun and moon stood still. Hab. 3:11
The universe shared in the battle for good.

Thou didst walk through the sea with thine horses. Hab. 3:15
The Lord guided them with His power.

ZEPHANIAH

The day of the Lord is at hand. Zeph. 1:7
The day of judgment; reckoning is nigh.

Pure language. Zeph. 3:9
A language of pure speech devoid of falsehood and deception.

HAGGAI

Bag with holes. Hag. 1:6
Money unwisely spent; hole in his pocket.

Heaven stayed from dew. Hag. 1:10
No rain came.

I will make thee as a signet. Hag. 2:23
I will give you authority and power.

ZECHARIAH

Red horse. Zech. 1:8
Bloodshed.

Speckled horse. Zech. 1:8
Famine, uncertainty.

White horse. Zech. 1:8
Victory.

Four horns. Zech. 1:18
Four powers.

Cattle in the city. Zech. 2:4
Material prosperity.

Call every man his neighbor under the vine and fig tree. Zech. 3:10
Symbolical of peace and harmony.

Two olive trees. Zech. 4:3
Two good and righteous leaders. (Zerubbabel and Joshua.)

Mountain. Zech. 4:7
A difficult task.

A flying scroll. Zech. 5:1
A hasty edict, decree.

Wind in the wings. Zech. 5:9
Speed and lifting power.

Quieted my spirit. Zech. 6:8
They satisfied my desire.

Take hold of skirt. Zech. 8:23
Beg for mercy, implore.

Riding upon an ass. Zech. 9:9
Humility, meekness.

I will sow them among the people. Zech. 10:9
I will scatter them among the nations.

Passing through the sea with affliction. Zech. 10:11
Going through life with difficulties.

They shall walk up and down in his name. Zech. 10:12
> *They shall be loyal to God's religion.*

Feed the flock. Zech. 11:4
> *Take care of the people.*

Cup of trembling. Zech. 12:2
> *Death.*

A burdensome stone. Zech. 12:3
> *A stumbling block.*

A fountain. Zech. 13:1
> *The truth; the new teaching.*

Cold and ice. (Lamsa) Zech. 14:6
> *Hardships and persecutions.*

Living water. Zech. 14:8
> *True religion.*

MALACHI

Spread dung upon your faces. Mal. 2:3
> *Cause you to be ashamed.*

Covering the altar with tears. Mal. 2:13
> *Weeping bitterly while offering gifts to God. Repentance.*

Refiner's fire and fuller's soap. Mal. 3:2
> *He will remove evil from among the people.*

They shall be ashes under the soles of your feet. Mal. 4:3
> *They shall be reduced to nothing.*

THE GOSPEL ACCORDING TO ST. MATTHEW

He knew her not. Matt. 1:19
> *He had not had intercourse with her.*

A virgin. Matt. 1:23
 A girl who has known no man; an unmarried woman.

Following the star. Matt. 2:9
 Walking in the direction of the stars.

Generation of vipers (scorpions). Matt. 3:7
 Sly, deceptive.

Baptism of fire. Matt. 3:11
 A thorough cleansing.

Untying another man's shoes. Matt. 3:16
 Respect and meekness.

Heavens were open. Matt. 3:16
 The heavens were receptive; a revelation.

Spirit descending like a dove. Matt. 3:16
 Signifies commission and meekness.

Angels ministered to him. Matt. 4:11
 Being comforted by God's thoughts, God's messengers.

He openeth his mouth. Matt. 5:2
 He broke the silence.

Poor in spirit. Matt. 5:3
 Poor in pride, humble.

Meek. Matt. 5:5
 Kindly disposed; bending.

Pure in heart. Matt. 5:8
 Pure in mind.

Salt of the earth. Matt. 5:13
 The flavor of this world; good conduct.

Raca. Matt. 5:22
 To spit.

Hell fire. Matt. 5:22
 Mental suffering; torment.

If thy right eye offend thee pluck it out. Matt. 5:29
> *If you have a habit of envying, cut it out. Stop it.*

Cut your hand off. Matt. 5:30
> *Stop stealing.*

Whosoever shall smite thee on thy right cheek, turn to him the other also. Matt. 5:39
> *Don't start a quarrel or fight. Be humble.*

Be ye perfect. Matt. 5:48
> *All inclusive. To know all lines of a trade. (See Gospel Light.)*

Let not thy left hand know what thy right hand doeth. Matt. 6:3
> *Don't advertise your giving.*

Closet. Matt. 6:6
> *Inner heart or mind.*

Treasure in heaven. Matt. 6:20
> *Good deeds recorded in heaven.*

Judge not. Matt. 7:1
> *Do not criticize.*

Pearls before swine. Matt. 7:6
> *Wise sayings before fools.*

By their fruit you shall know them. Matt. 7:16
> *By their works you shall know them.*

Good tree. Matt. 7:17
> *A good man.*

Corrupt tree. Matt. 7:17
> *An evil man.*

Bury my father. Matt. 8:21
> *Take care of my father until he dies.*

Devils besought him. Matt. 8:31
> *The insane men besought him.*

Going away into the swine. Matt. 8:31
To attack the herd of swine.

New cloth unto an old garment. Matt. 9:16
New teaching mixed with the old one.

New wine into old bottles (skins—Lamsa). Matt. 9:17
New teaching mixed with the old teaching.

Sheep without a shepherd. Matt. 9:36
People without a leader.

The way of the Gentiles. Matt. 10:5
Pagan practices.

The lost sheep. Matt. 10:6
The lost tribes of Israel. Lost men and women.

Shake off the sand from your feet. Matt. 10:14
Have nothing to do with them; leave them alone.

Sheep in the midst of wolves. Matt. 10:16
Good people among evil leaders.

Wise as serpents. Matt. 10:16
Avoid trouble.

Harmless as doves. Matt. 10:16
Trustful, pure in heart.

To bring a sword. Matt. 10:34
To bring division.

Take up the cross. Matt. 10:38
Willing to die, risk your life.

Born of a woman. Matt. 11:11
A human being with limitations, weaknesses.

We have piped to you. Matt. 11:17
We have tried to inform, to induce you to come out.

Eating and drinking. Matt. 11:19
Living comfortably.

My burden is light. Matt. 11:29
> *My religion is simple and easy. My demands are few.*

My yoke is easy. Matt. 11:29
> *My rule is easy.*

Any idle word. Matt. 12:36
> *A meaningless word; gossip.*

An unclean spirit. Matt. 12:43
> *An evil inclination; a demented person.*

Kingdom of heaven. Matt. 13:24
> *A universal state; a reign of peace and harmony.*

Wheat and tares. Matt. 13:25
> *Good people and bad people.*

Pearl of great price. Matt. 13:46
> *A great truth.*

Plant. Matt. 15:13
> *Teaching, doctrine.*

To take children's bread and cast it to dogs. Matt. 15:26
> *Sharing the truths of Judaism with the pagans.*

Leaven of the Pharisees. Matt. 16:6
> *Teaching of the Pharisees.*

Hell (Sheol—Lamsa). Matt. 16:6
> *A resting place for the departed ones.*

Gates of hell. Matt. 16:18
> *Evil forces; opposition.*

Upon this stone. Matt. 16:18
> *Upon this truth.*

The keys. Matt. 16:19
> *Authority, power.*

Keys of the Kingdom. Matt. 16:19
> *Spiritual authority.*

Shekel in the mouth of the fish. Matt. 17:27
> *A fish worth a shekel.*

If thy hand or foot offend thee, cut them off. Matt. 18:8
> *Stop stealing. Stop trespassing.*

If two of you shall agree. Matt. 18:19
> *If two of you are worthy.*

In His name. Matt. 18:20
> *In His method, His religion; His approach to God.*

If thou wilt be perfect. Matt. 19:21
> *All inclusive; thorough in every way.*

Rope in the eye of the needle. (Lamsa) Matt. 19:24
> *With great difficulty. (The rich man must give up something.)*

Is thine eye evil? Matt. 20:15
> *Are you envious or jealous?*

My cup you shall drink. Matt. 20:23
> *You shall die as I die.*

Riding on an ass. Matt. 21:5
> *Humble, meek.*

Removing mountains. Matt. 21:21
> *Overcoming seemingly unsurmountable difficulties and problems.*

Stone which the builders rejected. Matt. 21:42
> *Truth which religious men rejected.*

Like the angels of God. Matt. 22:30
> *Spiritual, pure, pious.*

A child of hell. Matt. 23:15
> *A corrupt person.*

Fill up the measure of your father. Matt. 23:32
> *You are as evil as your father.*

Coming in the name of the Lord. Matt. 23:39
> *An ambassador or a messenger of the Lord.*

Carcass and eagles (vultures—Lamsa). Matt. 24:28
  Weak nations and powerful nations.

Sheep and goats. Matt. 25:42
  Good people and bad people.

Sheep separated from goats. Matt. 25:33
  Good men separated from evil men.

The cup. Matt. 26:27
  The conspiracy; death.

Fruit of the vine. Matt. 26:29
  Joy.

Son of man. Matt. 26:64
  A human being; a man born of woman.

Right hand of power. Matt. 26:64
  Entrusted with power.

Coming on the clouds of heaven. Matt. 26:64
  The coming with glory, honor and victory.

The field of blood. Matt. 27:8
  Purchased with blood money.

Held him by his feet. Matt. 28:9
  Implored him.

THE GOSPEL ACCORDING TO ST. MARK

Kingdom of God. Mark 1:15
  God's counsel; a reign of harmony.

Repent ye. Mark 1:15
  Do not do it again.

He suffered not the devils to speak. Mark 1:34
  He did not allow the insane to speak after he had healed them.

My name is legion. Mark 5:9
  I have many wrong ideas; I am a hopeless case.

Send us into the swine. Mark 5:12
Let us attack the herd of swine.

Touch his garment. Mark 5:30
An urgent need.

Staff. Mark 6:8
Protection.

Corban. Mark 7:11
My sacrifice; a token of love and devotion.

Cast devil out of her daughter. Mark 7:26
He restored her daughter to sanity.

Dumb and deaf spirit. Mark 9:25
A man suffering from dumbness and deafness.

Foul spirit. Mark 9:25
A bad temper; an evil inclination.

Have salt in yourselves. Mark 9:50
Have good manners; good conduct.

Eat my body. Mark 14:22
Share my suffering. Make my teaching a part of you. Think of me when you celebrate the Passover.

Drink my blood. Mark 14:24
Make my teaching a part of your life. Be willing to suffer for my truth. Think of me when you celebrate the Passover.

Speak with new tongues. Mark 16:17
You will learn foreign languages wherever you go.

Take up a serpent. Mark 16:18
Handle an enemy; overcome opposition.

Drink any deadly thing. Mark 16:18
To be able to withstand any attacks against your character.

Amen. Mark 16:20
An oral seal; faithful, sincere and truthful.

THE GOSPEL ACCORDING TO ST. LUKE

Horn. Luke 1:69
Strength and triumph.

Valleys filled up. Luke 3:5
Wrongs righted, injustices removed.

Mountains and hills leveled. Luke 3:5
Proud and arrogant men humbled.

Crooked places made straight. Luke 3:5
Crooked teachings replaced by the truth.

Offspring of scorpions. Luke 3:37
Subtle and deceptive men.

Devils came out of men. Luke 4:41
Many insane men were restored.

Old and new wine. Luke 5:39
Judaism and Jesus' teaching.

Seven devils. Luke 8:2
Seven bad habits, wrong inclinations.

Shall not taste death. Luke 9:27
Shall not die spiritually.

Looking back. Luke 9:62
A lazy worker.

Do not know of what spirit you are. Luke 9:55
You don't realize what kind of temper you have.

Satan. Luke 10:18
To stay, to slide, to mislead, to slip; to miss the mark.

Satan falling. Luke 10:18
Evil destroyed.

Tread upon serpents. Luke 10:19
To overcome enemies and opposition.

Names written in heaven. Luke 10:20
You will be rewarded, your deeds are never to be forgotten.

Key of knowledge. Luke 11:52
Access to knowledge.

Little flock. Luke 12:32
A small group of believers.

Set the earth on fire. Luke 12:49
Upsetting the order of the day; revolutionizing the world.

Blood mingled with the sacrifices. Luke 13:1
Slain at the same time with their animal offerings.

Fox. Luke 13:32
Shrewd and subtle.

Eat bread in the Kingdom of God. Luke 14:15
Welcomed in the Kingdom of God.

Compel them to come. Luke 14:23
Urge them and beg them to come.

Mammon of the world. Luke 16:9
Money and other material things.

Sift you as wheat. Luke 22:31
Test you and purify you.

Sell your garment and buy a sword. Luke 22:36
Danger is imminent.

Sweat turned into blood. Luke 22:44
Greatly distressed; tense; in agony.

Right hand of God. Luke 22:69
Trust and power.

Green and dry tree. Luke 23:31
Green tree—an innocent man. Dry tree—an evil man.

Paradise. Luke 23:43
> *A Persian word for a beautiful garden; a place of harmony and tranquillity.*

THE GOSPEL ACCORDING TO ST. JOHN

Word. John 1:1
> *An utterance, a command.*

The only begotten son. John 1:18
> *The first one who recognized the fatherhood of God. The only God-like man; hence, a spiritual Son of God.*

In the bosom of the Father. John 1:18
> *Very close to Father—God.*

The lamb of God. John 1:29
> *Dedicated to God, innocent and blameless.*

The Messiah. John 1:41
> *The anointed one; ordained, commissioned.*

I saw thee under the fig tree. John 1:48
> *I have known you always.*

Angels of God ascending and descending. John 1:51
> *Understanding between God and man; reconciliation.*

Zeal eaten me up. John 2:17
> *Made me courageous.*

Destroy this temple and in three days I will raise it up. John 2:19.
> *Destroy the Jewish religion and I will rebuild it. Destroy my body and I will rise up in three days.*

Born again. John 3:3
> *To become like a child; to start all over.*

To set his seal. John 3:33
> *Approval of an act.*

Living water. John 4:11
True teaching.

One soweth and another reapeth. John 4:37
One works hard, another enjoys the fruits of his labor.

Manna. John 6:31
"Manna" means "what is it?" (It is like coriander seed, sweet like honey.)

Bread of life. John 6:35
Eternal truth.

Let him come to me and drink. John 7:37
Let him come and learn from me.

Rivers flow from the belly. John 7:38
Abundant and eternal truth. Spiritual satisfaction.

Writing on the ground. John 8:6
Doodling.

Darkness. John 8:19
Ignorance and superstition.

Thou hast a devil. John 8:48
You are crazy.

The bread of life. John 9:35
The true and eternal teaching.

Fell down at his feet. John 11:32
Paid him homage.

Let not your heart be troubled. John 14:1
Do not worry.

House of many mansions (many rooms—Lamsa). John 14:2
A kingdom for all races and peoples.

I am the true vine. John 15:1
I am the true religion.

He breathed on them. John 20:22
>   *He gave them courage.*

Feed my lambs. John 21:15
>   *Feed my young people, take care of them.*

Feed my sheep. John 21:16
>   *Feed the adults.*

Feed my ewes. (Lamsa) John 21:17
>   *Feed the young women.*

THE ACTS OF THE APOSTLES

Taken up. Acts 1:9
>   *Glorified, ascended.*

A cloud received him. Acts 1:9
>   *Welcome with glory and honor.*

Angel. Acts 1:10
>   *God's counsel, a messenger.*

Speaking in tongues. Acts 2:6
>   *Speaking in different dialects. (Aramaic and Hebrew, some of which were little understood.)*

Breaking bread. Acts 2:42
>   *At peace together.*

At the feet of the apostles. Acts 4:37
>   *Gifts given with no strings attached.*

Laid their hands on them. Acts 6:6
>   *Ordained them. (It also means to detain and accuse.)*

At the young man's feet. Acts 7:58
>   *Under his care.*

The Spirit of the Lord caught away Philip. Acts 8:39
>   *He was led by the Spirit of God to leave quickly.*

Kick against the pricks. Acts 9:5
To hurt one's self.

Smitten by an angel. Acts 12:23
Stricken suddenly.

Rent their clothes. Acts 14:14
They were horrified; a sign of mourning.

Spirit suffered them not. Acts 16:7
They were warned by a vision.

Shook his raiment. Acts 18:6
Exonerated himself of further responsibility.

Bound in the spirit. Acts 20:22
Determined; made up his mind.

Hebrew tongue. Acts 21:40
Aramaic dialect spoken by the Jews.

Threw dust in the air. Acts 22:23
A sign of mourning; shocked.

Thou whited wall. Acts 23:3
You hypocrite.

THE EPISTLE OF PAUL TO THE ROMANS

God as a witness. Rom. 1:9
I am not lying.

Their throat is an open sepulchre. Rom. 3:13
They utter lies, and they are corrupt.

Table as a snare. Rom. 11:9
Let their conspiracy turn against themselves.

Heap coals of fire on their head. Rom. 12:20
Cause them to regret.

Laid down their necks. Rom. 16:4
Willing to work hard; to die for the truth.

Bruise Satan under your feet. Rom. 16:20
  Crush evil or error.

THE FIRST EPISTLE OF PAUL TO THE CORINTHIANS

Feed with milk. 1 Cor. 3:2
  Trained with simple teachings.

Ye have reigned like Kings. 1 Cor. 4:8
  You are very independent.

To deliver such a one to Satan. 1 Cor. 5:5
  To turn him over to his own evil.

A little leaven. 1 Cor. 5:6
  A little teaching; a little truth.

Tongues of angels. 1 Cor. 13:1
  Speech without deception; truthful.

Unknown tongue. 1 Cor. 14:2
  An alien tongue; a strange dialect; an ancient tongue.

Spirits of the prophets. 1 Cor. 14:32
  Gifts of prophecy.

Death, where is thy sting? 1 Cor. 15:55
  Death, where is your power?

THE SECOND EPISTLE OF PAUL
TO THE CORINTHIANS

A door was opened. 2 Cor. 2:12
  An opportunity came.

Open face. 2 Cor. 3:18
  Without blame; guiltless.

From glory to glory. 2 Cor. 3:18
  Highly honored.

Our mouth is open. 2 Cor. 6:11
> *We have told you everything and we have hidden nothing.*

Heart is enlarged. 2 Cor. 6:11
> *I am relieved.*

Filthiness of the spirit. 2 Cor. 7:1
> *Evil inclination.*

Thorn in the flesh. 2 Cor. 12:7
> *Grievance; annoyance.*

THE EPISTLE OF PAUL TO THE GALATIANS

Angel from heaven. Gal. 1:8
> *Teacher of religion.*

For every man shall bear his own burden. Gal. 6:5
> *Let every man solve his own problem.*

THE EPISTLE OF PAUL TO THE EPHESIANS

The prisoner of the Lord. Eph. 4:1
> *A prisoner on account of being a follower of Jesus.*

Have your feet shod. Eph. 6:15
> *Be alert; ready.*

THE EPISTLE OF PAUL TO THE PHILIPPIANS

Bowels. Phil. 1:8
> *Heart.*

Beware of dogs. Phil. 3:2
> *Beware of gossipers and troublemakers.*

Trust in the flesh. Phil. 3:4
> *Trust in man-made teachings and ordinances; trust in the arm of man.*

THE EPISTLE OF PAUL TO THE COLOSSIANS

With you in spirit. Col. 2:5
Spiritually I am with you. (Spirit means all-embracing.)

Walk in Him. Col. 2:6
Follow His religion, His teaching.

Buried with Him in baptism. Col. 2:12
Regenerated; cleansed.

Mortify your members. Col. 3:5
Bring your members under control.

THE FIRST EPISTLE OF PAUL
TO THE THESSALONIANS

God is witness. 1 Thes. 2:5
What I am saying is true.

Lifting of hands. 1 Thes. 2:6
Imploring God in prayer.

Satan hindered us. 1 Thes. 2:18
Opposition hindered us; adversity.

For now we live. 1 Thes. 3:8
Now we rejoice.

To meet Him in the air. 1 Thes. 4:17
To hasten to greet Him.

THE FIRST EPISTLE OF PAUL TO TIMOTHY

Delivered unto Satan. 1 Tim. 1:20
I washed my hands of them; let them suffer for their own evil devices.

Spirit speaketh. 1 Tim. 4:1
Prophecy.

Doctrines of devils. 1 Tim. 4:1
> *Erroneous teachings.*

Lay hands on no man. 1 Tim. 5:22
> *Do not ordain any man. (It also means do not accuse any man falsely.)*

THE SECOND EPISTLE OF PAUL TO TIMOTHY

Snare of the Devil. 2 Tim. 2:26
> *Evil, pagan practices.*

THE EPISTLE OF PAUL TO TITUS

Evil beasts with slow bellies (empty bellies—Lamsa). Titus 1:12
> *Vicious men hungry for power; greedy.*

THE EPISTLE OF PAUL TO PHILEMON

Put that on mine account. Phil. 1:18
> *Forget it.*

THE EPISTLE OF PAUL TO THE HEBREWS

Flame of fire. Heb. 1:17
> *Speed, power and prompt action; fluency in speech.*

Oil of gladness. Heb. 1:9
> *I have ordained you with joy.*

Swore in my wrath. Heb. 3:11
> *I swore in my anger.*

Two edged sword. Heb. 4:12
> *The Word of God is like a double-edged sword which cuts both ways.*

Milk—strong meat. Heb. 5:12
> *Milk—simple teaching. Strong meat—doctrines and dogmas.*

Blood of the testament. Heb. 9:20
A solemn agreement sealed with blood.

Entertaining angels. Heb. 13:2
Entertaining pious or holy men.

The fruit of our lips. Heb. 13:15
Thanksgiving offered to God through prayer.

THE EPISTLE OF JAMES

Beholding face in a glass. Jas. 1:23
Unreality.

Devils tremble. Jas. 2:19
The insane ungodly men are afraid.

Tongue is a fire. Jas. 3:6
Powerful, fluent.

THE FIRST EPISTLE OF PETER

Living stone. 1 Pet. 2:4
Strong, good men and women worthy to be in the church of God.

Chief shepherd. 1 Pet. 5:4
The leader of the Church.

THE SECOND EPISTLE OF PETER

Angels. 2 Pet. 2:4
Ministers; ambassadors of God.

Wells without water. 2 Pet. 2:17
False teachers.

Dog is turned to his own vomit. 2 Pet. 2:22
A man who repeats his mistakes.

THE FIRST EPISTLE OF JOHN

Born of God. 1 John 3:9
God-like, holy; one who has repented from evil.

My little children. 1 John 2:1
My dear ones; my beloved.

Spirits. 1 John 4:1
Prophecies.

Spirit that confesseth. 1 John 4:2
True prophecies; true persons who confess the truth.

THE REVELATION OF ST. JOHN THE DIVINE

Seven spirits. Rev. 1:4
Seven Churches.

With cloud. Rev. 1:7
With glory.

Aleph and Tau. (Lamsa) Rev. 1:8
The first and the last; the beginning and the end.

Seven candlesticks. Rev. 1:12
Seven lights of the truth; seven Churches.

Golden girdle. Rev. 1:13
Kingly power.

Fiery eyes. Rev. 1:14
Beautiful, attractive and sincere.

White. Rev. 1:14
Purity and innocence.

Feet like unto brass. Rev. 1:15
Strong.

Seven stars. Rev. 1:16
Seven planets; symbolical of the seven Churches.

Was dead, alive forevermore. Rev. 1:18
I was unknown and now I am well known and successful.

To the angel. Rev. 2:1
To the minister.

Tree of life. Rev. 2:7
Eternal life.

Sword of the mouth. Rev. 2:16
The truth which exposes and destroys error.

Hidden manna. Rev. 2:17
Hidden truth.

White stone. Rev. 2:17
A distinguished person. (His name is engraved upon a white stone, a lasting memorial.)

Rod of iron. Rev. 2:27
Strong discipline.

Thou livest and art dead. Rev. 3:1
You are finished, useless.

An open door. Rev. 3:8
An opportunity.

I was in the spirit. Rev. 4:2
I saw a vision.

White horse. Rev. 6:2
Victory.

Red horse. Rev. 6:4
Bloodshed.

Black horse. Rev. 6:5
Death.

Pale horse. Rev. 6:8
Famine.

Four angels. Rev. 7:1
Four of God's messengers; messages.

Washed their robes in blood. Rev. 7:14
Martyred.

Living waters. Rev. 7:17
Eternal life—truth.

Sun and air darkened by smoke. Rev. 7:18
Impending catastrophe; confusion.

Clothed in a cloud. Rev. 10:1
Gloriously arrayed.

Take the little book and eat it. Rev. 10:9
Remember it by heart; make it a part of you.

Sweet in my mouth like honey. Rev. 10:10
I was overcome by the secret which the book contained.

My belly was bitter. Rev. 10:10
I could not impart the secret.

The dragon. Rev. 12:13
Evil forces; adversary—opposition to the truth. Also a dictator.

Ten horns. Rev. 13:1
Ten kings.

The number of the beast 666. Rev. 13:18
Nero Caesar. (Aramaic—Nron Ksr 666)

Temple filled with smoke. Rev. 15:8
God's reverence greatly felt.

Keepeth his garments. Rev. 16:15
Alertness.

Angel standing in the sun. Rev. 19:17
An announcement made openly.

Satan loosed. Rev. 20:7
Evil forces become dominant.

Twelve foundations. Rev. 21:14
>   *The teaching of the twelve apostles.*

Twelve pearls. Rev. 21:21
>   *Twelve fundamental truths.*

Tree of life. Rev. 22:2
>   *Perfect man; perfect humanity.*

Dogs. Rev. 22:15
>   *Vicious men; gossipers.*

The bright and morning star. Rev. 22:16
>   *The dawning of the truth.*

Part Two

A Key to the Original Gospel

The Language of Jesus

Jesus and His disciples only spoke Aramaic and preached to simple and poor people who could understand them. Latin was spoken by Roman officials and Jews who were attached to the court of the Roman Governor. Greek was understood by a few cultured business men and merchants. The masses spoke Aramaic. Even Jewish writings, prior to this time, such as sacred biblical literature, were found in Aramaic. The Hebrew scriptures were interpreted by the priests and lawyers in Aramaic. Centuries after the Christian Era we still find Jewish writings, such as the Talmud and Mishna in Aramaic.

Indeed the Jews despised both the Greeks and the Romans. The racial antipathy was so bitter because both Romans and Greeks were non-Semites and their customs and religions too alien to those of the Jews. The Greeks had conquered them and massacred many of their numbers. The marks of suffering which the Jews had borne during the Greek period were still to be seen. The Romans were just beginning to subjugate them.

On the other hand, early Christianity was nothing more than perfected Judaism, inspired with Jewish traditions and hopes. As long as Christianity remained a Jewish movement, thus appealing to the Jewish racial aspirations and Jewish thought, the Jews continued to champion its cause. In the second century A.D. the Jews saw that Pagan customs, Greek and Egyptian traditions and religious commercialism were creeping into Christianity. Doctrines and dogmas were replacing the teaching of Jesus and those of the Prophets, and there was danger of Jewish amalgamation with Gentiles. Therefore the Jews dropped their interest, and took no more part in what was then known as a Gentile movement.

Both Greeks and Romans were brought into the fold of Christianity by the Jewish and Syrian missionaries when the Christian Church became strong in Judea and Syria. Therefore, the original Gospels were written only for the Jews and in the

language of the Jewish people and the Syrians who spoke
Aramaic. The style of writing, the manner of speech and compo-
sition are purely Aramaic and not easily translated into other
languages. It is not so with the Epistles of St. Paul. There, I find
Aramaic thought and manner of speech dictated into Greek.

In order to illustrate this point more clearly, I will take for
example the Armenian and Assyrian races, both conquered by
the Turks, and who, for nearly six hundred years passed through
experiences and persecutions alike to those of the Jews. Neither
of these two races lost their language nor did they encourage the
Turkish language, either in business or in the home. They never
wrote books in Turkish, especially sacred literature, which the
Easterners believed would be defiled if written in the language
of a conquering race which had oppressed its people. On the
other hand, the Greek conquest of Palestine did not last very
long. The Jews continuously fought Greek domination and fi-
nally succeeded in gaining their independence under the Mac-
cabean kings. During this period the Jews persistently retained
their institutions, customs and language.

Another illustration is that of Christian Science. Mrs. Baker
Eddy being born in America spoke English, and preached in
English to English-speaking people. At the outset her teachings
were condemned. Who cared to translate her writings into other
languages? Who thought anything about it but the sick and who
were then known as lunatics? Who believed this sect would
attain such dramatic success? For many years Christian Science
writings were only printed in English.

Now let us suppose that all English texts of *Science and Health*
in the United States and England were burned, and a new translation made from Chinese into English, we would still have no
grounds to doubt that the original texts of Mrs. Eddy's *Science
and Health* might be discovered in Australia, nor could we think
that her works were originally written in Chinese, even though
we had in our possession a translation from Chinese which was
being used in common. Yet a translation of her work from Chinese into English would greatly differ from the original text.

The chief difficulties which the Westerner confronts in his

studies of the Gospels are the arrangement of the early writings —the writers and the language in which the writers thought, wrote and spoke. The documentary evidences which would solve most of these mysteries have perished, buried or lost, and the legendary information on which most of the textual criticism is built creates confusion. Therefore I believe the only way to penetrate these long and obscure centuries between the present advanced age in which we live and the simple age in which the Gospels were written is to explore virgin Eastern sources and to study Christianity from the Eastern point of view. We must also try to trace back into the language Jesus spoke some of His sayings and understand them in the light they were written. Then translate them through our modern thought into English.

Indeed scholarship has contributed generously through the discoveries of ancient peoples, tablets, and relics which enlighten us and help us to understand the past and left the way open for us to do the rest. On the other hand, the missions have made their greatest contribution towards scholarship by producing native scholars who not only understand the background and the language which Jesus and His Apostles spoke, but who also read, write and speak English.

Thus, in order to gain a thorough understanding of the original Gospels we have to study the development of Christianity in the Eastern Empire (Persia), and the fragmentary portions of the early Christian Church in the East which have survived persecutions and the rapid changes and modifications under successive dynasties.

Take for example, the Assyrian Church, founded in the early part of the first century A.D., and for many centuries the strongest branch of the Christian Church in the East and in fact, in the world. At present still using the Aramaic language and maintaining the early apostolic customs in practice and worship. In that part of the world we still live under an older civilization, a civilization from which Christian religion and its culture sprang. Our marital customs are the same as they were during the time of Jacob. We still pay a dower to the father of the bride, either in money, oxen or sheep. We still thrash wheat with oxen with their mouths tied. Two women, one young and one old, sit down grinding the wheat. We still use sheepskins for wine bottles, anoint with sacred oil, believe in the angelic visitation, see visions, sacrifice in high places and still practice Mosaic law. Our houses are built the same style as those of our ancestors who lived before Jesus. Our food and wearing apparel have never changed. Indeed in Assyria, time does not exist. When we think of Abraham and Moses, it looks as if they died but a month ago. Jesus seemed to have lived but a short while ago. These customs which seem to look so strange and ancient to an American, if discussed fully and studied carefully will obviously have a very strong influence on the fundamental structure and interpretation of the Gospels.

All the teachings of Jesus and His parables are illustrated only by the life and customs which were once in use in Northern Palestine but now only kept by the Assyrians. Jesus never went to Greece, India or Egypt. He said nothing about the customs of those countries, and there is nothing to indicate that He was anywhere outside of Palestine.

Aramaic Phraseology

The Aramaic language is simple in its manner of speech, but hard and peculiar in its expressions. Often a word is used which has many different meanings. Whereas Greek and Latin have many words to describe one thing. Moreover, there are idioms in Aramaic that can never be translated accurately into another language.

Aramaic conversation is strange. The speech is amplified as far as imagination can reach, in order to convey the thought; the object is magnified to many times its size in order to make persons see all its sides. In this way, the speech becomes persuasive and the power which radiates from its magnetic force shatters the doubts in the minds of listeners. Objects change; values increase and decrease; the harm which the glance of an eye to the body of a woman can cause is worse than the loss of an eye. In order to do this, facts become exaggerated: for example, Saul and David instead of killing a few hundred men, we say, they killed tens of thousands. A small army of fifty thousand is increased numerically, as the sands on the shores of the seas and the stars in the skies.

The Aramaic language has another method of conversation, which is used generally.

"If you can build that house in two months, I will kill myself." This means, "The task can never be accomplished."

"If you can buy this pair of shoes for less than two dollars, I will change myself into a donkey." This means—that the shoes cannot be bought for less.

"If you marry that woman, I will cut off my right arm." This means—it is an impossibility.

"If I don't tell the truth, you can pluck out my eye." This means—what I say is true.

"If I married that beautiful girl, I would never die." This means—the happiness of the marriage eliminates the thought of the death.

"We have eaten the flesh and drunk the blood of our fathers while building this house." This means, I have worked very hard to build this house.

"While doing this work I saw my dead people before my eyes." It means the task was almost impossible.

"I have eaten the flesh of my dead people." It means I have done hard work.

"I am going away, please do not cut your eyes from my wife and children." This means, take care of them while I am away.

"Your eyes are not carrying a burden." This means, you are jealous.

"My boy is sick because he has been hit by a woman's eye." This means, that a woman had envied the child.

"Abraham has given birth to many sheep, oxen and donkeys

because God has blessed him." This means, Abraham has been blessed by God, his sheep, oxen and donkeys have been increased.

"God holds you." This means God condemns you.

"Do not hurt that man, he is a man of God." It means he is a meek man.

"I and my father are one." This means that my father and I agree.

"Hold that highway in your hand until you come to the city." This means, that street will take you to the city.

"They laid hands on them." This means, they were detained and also means they were ordained.

"My heart is aching." This means, I have stomach trouble.

Aramaic in Palestine

In the Seventh Century B.C., Esarhaddon, Assyrian Emperor, carried the ten tribes of Israel captive to Assyria and replaced them by a mixed Assyrian population which rehabilitated Samaria and Galilee and the Assyrian dialect of the Northern Aramaic became the language of Galilee.* These Assyrians worshipped Jehovah, God of Israel, but the Jews always looked upon them as foreigners. Nothing could provoke the indignation of the Jews more than a Galilean aspiring to sit on the promised throne of David.

"For the children of Israel walked in all the sins of Jeroboam which he did; they departed not from them;

"Until the Lord removed Israel out of his sight, as he had said by all his servants the prophets. So was Israel carried away out of their own land to Assyria unto this day.

"And the king of Assyria brought men from Babylon, and from Cuthah, and from Ave, and from Hamath, and from Sepharvaim, and

---

*Hebrew is a branch of Aramaic, known as Western Aramaic. Abraham was an Assyrian. Isaac and Jacob married from Assyria and eleven of the sons of Jacob were born at the house of his uncle in Padanaram.

placed them in the cities of Samaria instead of the children of Israel; and they possessed Samaria, and dwelt in the cities thereof."

2 Kings 17–25.

"Now when the adversaries of Judah and Benjamin heard that the children of the captivity builded the temple unto the Lord God of Israel;

"Then they came to Zerubbabel, and to the chief of the fathers, and said unto them, Let us build with you: for we seek your God, as ye do; and we do sacrifice unto him since the days of Esar-haddon king of Assur, which brought us up hither.

"But Zerubbabel, and Jeshua and the rest of the chief of the fathers of Israel, said unto them, Ye have nothing to do with us to build a house unto our God, but we ourselves together will build unto the Lord God of Israel, as king Cyrus of Persia hath commanded us."

Ezra 4: 1–4.

Prior to the conquest of Judea by Nebuchadnezzer the Assyrian influence was spread all over Palestine, Judah became a tributary and the Assyrian language was spoken by princes and noblemen.

"Now therefore, I pray thee, give pledges to my lord the king of Assyria, and I will deliver thee two thousand horses, if thou be able on thy part to set riders upon them.

"How then wilt thou turn away the face of one captain of the least of my master's servants, and put thy trust on Egypt for chariots and for horsemen?

"Am I now come up without the Lord against this place to destroy it? The Lord said to me, Go up against this land, and destroy it.

"Then said Eliakim the son of Hilkiah, and Shebna, and Joah, unto Rab-shakeh, Speak, I pray thee, to thy servants in the Aramaic language; for we understand it: and talk not with us in the Jews' language in the ears of the people that are on the wall."

2 Kings 18: 23–27.

About 480 B.C., Nebuchadnezzer, King of Chaldeans, carried Judah captive to Babylon. When they had forgotten Hebrew, the Chaldean dialect, or Southern Aramaic, became their daily language. Apparently there are some peculiarities and differences in the phraseology and manner of speech in these two dialects even today. This is why the Jews in Jerusalem who spoke Southern Aramaic could not understand some of the parables and sayings which Jesus used in His Galilean or Northern Aramaic speech.

During the exile and the post-exile, Jewish sacred writings were in Aramaic. In the third century B.C., the Old Testament was translated into Greek, because the Alexandrian Jews could not understand Aramaic. This was done simply to facilitate the study of the scriptures among the Jews in Egypt where the Greek language predominated. But the Jews in Palestine, Mesopotamia and Persia confined their writings to Aramaic. An old Jewish colony in the Province of Aderbajan, Persia, still speaks and uses Aramaic. There are also other isolated Jewish settlements in Kurdistan and Turkey which are remnants of the Captivity, and who still speak and read Aramaic.

Authors

There is little historical evidence at our disposal to establish the identity of the authors of our Gospels, but we know that all the writers whoever they might have been were Jews and had been with Jesus.

The authors of the Gospels omitted their names from the documents they wrote just to hide their identity. The Government and ecclesiastical authorities would have done their utmost to arrest them and try them for treason, if they had been apprehended. Peter* began his epistle with his name because he was writing from Babylon and Babylon was in the Parthian-Persian Empire.

There is every reason to believe that the first writer of the Gospels was Matthew who was a Publican. In the East the qualification for the office of Publican is that he must read and write. A bishop and a priest do not necessarily have to know how to

---

* The general public belief has always been that Peter lived in the East and died in Babylon. The patriarch of the East had assumed the title "Mar-Shimun" (St. Peter) long before the bishop of Rome was recognized as head of the Church in the West.

read and write. Other disciples were illiterate, recruited from the ranks of fishermen and farmers. No other man who had not seen and heard Jesus could have quoted His sayings so accurately. Therefore, there is every indication that the writer is one who had been with Jesus and who knew how to write. Matthew wrote in Aramaic, the language of his people. Mark, Luke and John were also originally written in Aramaic.

Matthew wrote to the people who had seen and known Jesus. His material was confined to what he heard, saw and understood. Other Gospels were copied from Matthew, with supplementary information which the copyist had gathered from those who had known Jesus and heard about Him, and which Matthew had not considered very important. Even these latter accounts were in the common language which the people spoke. This was necessary as the first missionary work of the Church was among the Aramaic-speaking people. For years prior to the conversion of St. Paul, the Apostles preached to races whose language they understood and whose customs were similar to those of their own.

Sayings of Jesus

It was years after the Resurrection that the public began to inquire into the life and works of Jesus. The simple oral narrative which hitherto had been carried secretly from mouth to mouth spread very rapidly. Men and women quoted some of Jesus' sayings, and at times invoked His divine power. The demand for information concerning His life and teachings greatly increased.

At the outset a scribe supplied the public need with sayings of Jesus, written on parchment scrolls. The sacred writings which these scrolls contained were used for healing and protection from evil spirits. Indeed the public did not care for what the writer himself thought about Jesus. What they wanted was only what Jesus said.

Evidently, the early simple people were not looking for a critical commentary to find out whether Jesus was the Son of God or not, or to question His teachings. They wanted to treasure in their hearts, the divine and comforting words of their master. The words which had healed the sick, opened the eyes of the blind, cleansed the leper and proclaimed tidings of the Kingdom of Heaven on earth. What else did they want? All these early followers of Jesus believed in His divine power and accepted Him as the promised Messiah.

On the other hand, the writer did not care to write a complete biography of their Master as most of these people who wanted to possess the sacred writings had seen Jesus and known a great deal about Him.

The next generation began to inquire when, where, why and how Jesus did certain things. They had not seen Him and some of them wanted a stronger proof of His life than the mere writing of the scrolls which they read. Therefore, a new field of inquiry was opened. This time the public wanted a biography of Jesus. They wanted in writing something which the first writer had not considered very important and the first Christians had not considered wise to be incorporated in the Holy Sayings of their beloved Lord.

It is this later material which makes our present Gospels differ. Each writer seems to have copied Matthew's original work of the sayings of Christ with supplementary information which he had collected from men and women who had learned about Jesus from their parents. This is why one writer traces the genealogy of Jesus back to David by the way of Solomon. The other goes back to Adam through Nathan, son of David.

It is amazing to think that some of these later writers seem to know more about Jesus than He did Himself. Jesus did not seem to have known anything concerning this kingly ancestry. He never spoke a word about it. He never even said of what tribe of Israel He was from. He heard Pharisees and priests denouncing Him and repudiating His Messianic claims on the grounds that He was not from the House of David and that he was not born in Bethlehem. According to the Jewish tradition which strongly prevailed at the time of Jesus, the Messiah was to be born in Bethlehem and to be a descendant from the House of David.

"But many of the people who heard his words then said: Truly he is the Prophet.

"Has not the scripture said that from the seed of David and from Bethlehem, the town of David, Christ shall come? Others said, This is the Christ. But some said, Shall Christ come out of Galilee?"

St. John 7: 40–43.

"Nicodemus saith unto them (one of them he that came to Jesus by night),

"Doth our law convict man, before it hear him, and know what he had done?

"They answered and said unto him, why art you also of Galilee? Search, and look; for out of Galilee ariseth no prophet."

St. John 7: 50–53.

Moreover, Jesus heard people calling Him Samaritan but he never tried to contradict His enemies and to prove He was from the line of David. Instead he challenged the Jewish literal ecclesiastical opinion that Christ was to be a descendant from the line of David.

"While the Pharisees were gathered together, Jesus asked them,

"And he said, What do you say concerning Christ? whose son is he? They said unto him, The son of David.

"He said unto them, How then does David in spirit* call him Lord, because he said,

"The Lord said unto my Lord, Sit thou on my right hand, till I make thine enemies thy footstool.

"If David then call him Lord, how is he his son?"

St. Matthew 22: 41–46.

Here Jesus tried to show the Jews that they understood the scriptures; literally that Christ was not limited to any particular house or tribe, but that He could come from any tribe.

Apparently the disciples of Jesus who wrote the early documents knew that their Lord was rejected by the Jews because He was a Galilean and not a descendant of David. They heard Him

---

*Spirit here means prophetically.

debating this question and silenced His enemies. How could they have written the portions of our scriptures which accord to Jesus this distinctive Jewish Messianic claim?

This is what happened. The generation which had seen and known Jesus had passed away, His disciples, as well as His enemies also had died. The Jewish authorities had not written anything concerning Jesus because in their eyes He died on the cross. Therefore He was the accursed one. These writers were free to incorporate into the early writings the new material which they collected.

Therefore in order to find the connecting link to the original Gospels and to throw further light on the Gospel's history, we must look back through a long period of years in order to study varied documents and systems of copying work employed at times when scholarship and accuracy were least known, when each writer had his own method of spelling and when there were no grammarians; when writers were few, writing materials scarce, books rare and limited only to congregations and rich families who could well afford to possess such sacred material. At that time there was vigorous zeal displayed by the missionaries and followers of Jesus for expansion of Christianity, but little technique and less discipline and uniformity.

Moreover, we must also remember that at that time there were no scholars, no bishops nor popes to control the thought and suppress the writings. The main object of the Church in the East and West was to convert the Pagan world. Therefore for many centuries the Gospels were not compiled, and varied Syriac (Aramaic) texts were in use.

Eastern Versions

The Eastern Church in Persia had its own versions of the Gospels in Syro-Chaldean Aramaic. They were brought into the

East during the first century A.D. by the Apostle Addai* and
other disciples. These early documents were used by the church
in Persia many years before Marcian and Tatian were born. The
versions in common use in the East later were called "Peshitta
and Mkabalta" which means, the common (simple), and the
accepted one. "Peshitta" contains only twenty-two books, as the
Book of Revelation and a number of other epistles were not
accepted in the East until later on. A part of the ancient Assyrian
liturgy known as "Kodasha" of the Apostles and the oldest liturgy in the world uses the early Syriac versions. Moreover, these
versions differ extensively from those of the West. It is important to note that the Mohammedans only accept these Eastern
Gospels as authentic and charge that the Western texts were
forged. Therefore when a Christian takes oath by the Gospel it
is required that the book of "Engel" be one of the Eastern versions. Greek was never spoken in Mesopotamia and
Persia, while Aramaic dominated in Syria and Palestine. Thus
the change of the Gospels from Aramaic into Syro-Chaldean was
an easy task. The work was very simple because there was no
need for translation as the meaning of words in either language
was the same. The writer only had to change the Hebrew char-
acters into another style of slightly modified letters, known as
Syriac.

Early Translations

Christianity from its early start spread into the two powerful
and rival Empires, Persia and Rome. These two great powers for
centuries were engaged in warfare. It is highly important to note
that Christians in the Roman Empire passed through ten major
and severe persecutions which lasted for nearly 300 years and
at times threatened to almost obliterate the Church.

*Addai was one of the seventy who went out preaching.

The Christian property was confiscated and Christians looked upon as traitors to the Empire. Moreover, the mental energy of Christian leaders was absorbed by the thought to save Christianity. Doctrines, dogmas and sacred writings occupied little thought or none at all.

In the Persian Empire the state of affairs was different; for more than three centuries persecutions were unknown. Instead, Persia had become a refuge place for Christians who because of their faith were driven and banished from the Roman Empire.

When Constantine championed the cause of Christians and he, himself, became a convert, Persian policy toward Christianity in the East was suddenly changed. The Christians whom hitherto Persia had pitied, came to be looked upon as friends and spies of Rome. Assuredly, the three centuries of peace gave Eastern Christians time and opportunity to contribute much towards the development of the scriptures; to organize the Church and to establish Theological Schools. Tatian, the Assyrian, made a new "Diatesaron" version of the Gospels; later St. Ephrim wrote a commentary on the scriptures. Whereas, in the Roman Empire the conditions were different and the task of Christians hard. During all this period of peace and tranquillity in Persia, in the Roman Empire Christians were put to death, books and Churches destroyed and burned, Christian gatherings disbanded. The Christians in the West had no time to devote to scholarly research and writing. They had to be content with what survived the destruction. They had to copy the Gospels again and again hastily and, at times, from incomplete and damaged manuscripts.

After the expansion of Christianity among Semites, the Greeks were the first non-Semites to be converted. Therefore, the Greek translation of the Gospels was the first made from the original language. In all of the Greek and Latin versions we find that the early translators had left some of the Aramaic words untranslated. It seems likely that the translators did not agree on the meaning of certain Aramaic words. As some of these

words remained in the original Aramaic, they have a double
meaning.

For example: "Talita Komey," which means, "O, thou who
sleepest arise" and "Little girl arise." The word "talita" means
both little girl and sleep.

The Birth of Jesus

"But the birth of Jesus Christ was in this way, while Mary his
mother was 'Makhirta' (bought for a price) for Joseph, before he knew
her, she was found pregnant through the holy spirit. But Joseph, her
husband, was a quiet* man and did not let it be known, thinking to
divorce her secretly. While he was meditating over this the angel of
God appeared to him in a dream and said unto him: Joseph, son of
David, do not be afraid to take your wife Mary."

St. Matthew 1: 18.
(Literal translation from the Eastern version)

Among the people who still live according to the ancient
customs and are governed by unwritten laws, a marriage con-
tract is not binding until the price for the girl is paid in full. The
wedding follows soon after payment of the price, as in the East,
courtship with prospective brides is unknown. An engagement
is simply an informal announcement which the bridegroom's
parents make. Therefore the verbal agreement is temporary and
not binding to either party. Thus before the dower is paid the
sole jurisdiction over the prospective bride is that of her parents.
Jacob had no money or cattle to pay for his wives so he had to
work fourteen years for his Uncle Laban in order to marry two
of his uncle's daughters.

When the price of a bride is paid, she becomes automatically
responsible only to her husband whenever her conduct and
chastity are questioned. Her parents no longer have anything to

*A man who feared God.

say. There is one exception, which is so unusual and has been kept so sacred in the marital customs, and that is, that when a young girl who is under age is given in marriage, a verbal agreement is entered into between the parents of the parties concerned, especially when the bridegroom is a widower of an older age, or one who has more than one wife, the bridegroom should respect his newly wedded wife until she arrives at the age of maturity. In the East the marriageable age for girls is 12, but many girls, for various reasons, are given in marriage at the age of 7. The little bride dresses as a married woman. She performs her duty as a wife in all household affairs, and sleeps with her husband. But she is not consumed until she reaches the age of twelve. When the bride becomes a full-fledged wife her virginity is witnessed by two elderly women, and the token of her purity is kept.

"Then shall the father of the damsel, and her mother, take and bring forth the tokens of the damsel's virginity unto the elders of the city in the gate:

"And the damsel's father shall say unto the elders, I gave my daughter unto this man to wife, and he hateth her;"

Deut. 22: 15, 16.

From a study of the Eastern text of the Gospels and the Aramaic social customs, we see that Joseph and Mary were married. That is to say that Joseph had paid the price by which a husband becomes sole owner of his wife. But it seems very likely that Joseph had married a girl who was under age, while he was a middle-aged man. Mary is found pregnant through the Holy Spirit, and Joseph thinks that she committed adultery. Joseph was a God-fearing man. He tried to obtain a decree of divorce without letting the public know. To divorce her secretly—that is, to ask Mary's parents to return the dowry, on the grounds that their daughter was not a virgin, and then procure an annulment on some other grounds less criminal than adultery. According to the Jewish moral code, the punishment for adultery is death. The woman is stoned and the first stones are thrown by her own relatives.

"If a damsel that is a virgin be betrothed unto an husband, and a man finds her in the city, and lie with her;

"Then ye shall bring them both out unto the gate of that city, and ye shall stone them with stones that they die; the damsel, because she cried not, being in the city; and the man, because he hath humbled his neighbour's wife: so thou shalt put away evil from among you.

"If a man find a damsel that is a virgin, which is not betrothed, and lay hold on her, and lie with her, and they be found;

"Then the man that lay with her shall give unto the damsel's father fifty shekels of silver, and she shall be his wife; because he hath humbled her, he may not put her away all his days."

Deut. 22: 23, 24, 28, 29.

Therefore, if Mary was only betrothed, Joseph would have not known anything concerning her secret affairs; he would have had nothing to do with her affairs and there would have been no reason for divorce. It would have been for Mary's parents and the town to punish her. On the other hand, if Mary was not married she could not have escaped the severe punishment. No one would have believed that she had angelic visitations.

It is also of interest that according to Jewish law no illegitimate child could be brought to the temple and presented to God. Therefore if there had been the slightest suspicion of the legitimacy of Jesus His mother could not have presented Him at the temple.

Tried Out

"Then was Jesus carried away by the holy Spirit into the wilderness, to be tried out by the adversary."

St. Matthew 4: 1.
(Literal translation)

The word "dnethnasey" in this case means to be tried out. When an Easterner purchased an ox or a horse, he tried it out for a number of days.

Jesus was full of zeal and enthusiasm, but at the same time

was confronting opposition from His relatives, friends and enemies. His interpretation of the scriptures differed from that of
the scholars; and His outlook on religion created much opposition. They looked upon Him as a visionary—an unbalanced man
—a man who was possessed with the devil. Some discouraged
Him, others tried to persuade Him to quit His work, others
sought His life. He went to the desert to think these things over,
to see if He was the man or not. To find out if He had strength
to withstand the suffering which He might confront while
carrying on His great mission. There were other thoughts in
His mind: Can He work with high priests and elders? Can He
bring out what He intends to do without worshipping His
superiors?

Wedding at Cana

"What is it to me and to you, woman?" "Why should we
worry about the wine." "La dakel etat shaat." "My turn has not
come; other guests are before me who have yet to do their duty
before I can instruct the servants to bring wine. I will do it when
my turn comes." The gentle remarks exchanged between Mary
and Jesus were partly made by speech and partly by hands and
head, in order not to embarrass other guests. Mary's mind was
relieved. She told the servants to watch Jesus and when His turn
came, to do whatever He told them; if sent out to bring a few
jars of wine, to go. "Shaat" means also time and clock. The term
"woman" in Aramaic is addressed to a married woman.

Such was the picture of the wedding feast at Cana, where
Mary sat with a group of women, her face wreathed in smiles,
her eyes fastened on her beloved one. Her son was the only
one among the guests who had not drunk to excess. It would
have been truly oriental for Mary to have wished to see her son
a little drunk and active in the feast. Jesus had likely drunk a

few cups just to please the bridegroom and those sitting near Him.

Mary at times chatted with the women and discussed wedding affairs and the match, all agreeing, except the mother-in-law, that the bride was a hard worker and a good bargain.

The wedding festivities were gradually subsiding; the servants were standing idle; there was no more wine. Mary, thinking that Jesus' turn to treat the guests had come, made a sign with her eyes which told Him to bring wine for the guests. "Son, order the servants to bring some wine for the guests." She spoke to Him through the motion of her lips and the gesticulating of her hands. Other men had brought wine and made the feast merry, why should not her son do the same. She felt unhappy over the remarks of the women, servants and guests who praised so generously those who shared in making the feast a success. For a while Mary thought that her son was bashful, or that He was unfamiliar with the wedding customs, and, therefore, had not called on the servants to bring wine.

Peter

The word "Peter" is derived from the Aramaic word "Kepa," which means rock. Simon, the Aramaic being "Shimmon," means hearing, and is one of the most popular names among the Shemites. The name is a sacred one, given by a mother in answer to her prayer to God for a child. "God has hearkened to my voice." On the other hand, among the Aramaic-speaking people, "Kepa" (stone) has never been used for a name. All Semitic names have some religious meaning. Names such as stone, street, shoe, bridge, fox, if given to an Easterner, would cause him to commit murder.

The term "kepa" is a general nickname given to stupid people and to those who ask questions and pay little attention to what has been said. Peter "Kepa" is one of the most offensive of nicknames; a sword wound inflicted on the body of an Easterner would hurt less than the nickname "kepa" hurts the heart.

Jesus felt sorry for Simon when others teased him and called him "stone-headed." He knew how offended His countrymen were when given nicknames. He knew, moreover, that Simon did not understand easily. His rich mind was hard to cultivate, just as a field which has never been ploughed will, when cultivated, bear fruits. The joking having subsided, and Jesus finished speaking, He turned to Peter, smiling, and said, "Thou art the rock, and on this rock I will build my church." The Aramaic word for church is "eta"—group. Jesus wanted to cheer Peter, and to avoid a break between him and his partners because of his new and provoking name.

Raca

"But I say unto you, That whosoever is angry with his brother without a cause shall be in danger of the judgment: and whosoever shall say to his brother, Raca, shall be guilty to the council, and whosoever shall say, Thou effeminate one, shall be doomed to hell fire."

St. Matthew 5: 22.
(Literal translation from Aramaic)

"Raca"* in Aramaic means "to spit in one's face."

In the East, spitting in each other's face is done very frequently during the business hours and at times when persons enter into heated arguments. When a merchant and his prospective customer disagree in their bargaining, they generally spit in each other's face.

---

*Raca has never been translated into Greek or Latin. The translators were unable to understand its meaning.

To Him That Has It Shall Be Given

In Kurdistan and Assyria often a landlord divides his fields among his tenants to cultivate for him. The landlord provides the seed and equipment when necessary. In September, when the harvest is over, the wheat is divided into one-fifth for the landlord and four-fifths for his tenants. In case a tenant has not taken good care of his land and crops have been poor, the landlord takes all of the wheat his tenant has produced for his share and seed which he loaned. Then he turns the wheat and the land over to another tenant who has been more faithful and successful in cultivating the land.

The Rich Man

"Then said Jesus unto His disciples, Verily I say unto you, That a rich man shall hardly enter into the kingdom of heaven.

"And again I say unto you, It is easier for a camel to go through the eye of a needle, than for a rich man to enter into the Kingdom of God."

St. Matthew 19: 23, 24.

Jesus condemned the Eastern rich men and barred them from entering into the kingdom of heaven. Because a rich man acquires his wealth not so much by his profession or hard labor as by force and graft. The rich man harvests where he has not sown seed; he gathers from where he has not reaped; and by the virtue of his wealth becomes an overlord; too holy to bear the burdens like those borne by the common people of his town. According to Eastern traditions wealth is a blessing from God showered on those He loves. Nevertheless, most Easterners would never wait for God to bless them. They bless themselves simply by unjustly acquiring property belonging to the poor. The sooner they are blest the better it is. When God had made a man rich, "let us keep him rich," say the Easterners. On the other hand, the poor man is cursed; that is the reason why he is poor, and to help a poor man to become rich is against the will of God.

As soon as an Easterner acquires money, servants and lands, he is exempt from all local and federal taxes. Furthermore, through an oral law this rich man levies special taxes on the poor of his town whenever he pleases. When other rich men come to visit him, he kills the sheep of the poorest men in his town, to make a feast for his honorable guests.

The rich men are also beggars. They are the only ones who are permitted to collect money when their revenues fall short, or when they intend to add a few more women to their harems. Often you can see a stranger entering a certain town, accompanied by scores of armed servants, riding on beautiful horses. He is the Eastern rich man from another town who has come to beg. On his arrival, he is met and escorted to a rich man's house, who immediately begins to collect sheep, oxen and money from the poor of his town to be given to his friend. A poor man is allowed to beg only crumbs of bread which have been left at the tables.

Take No Money

"Provide neither gold, nor silver, nor brass in your purses;
"Nor scrip for your journey, neither two shirts, neither shoes, nor stave: for the workman is worthy of 'sebartha'—his food."

St. Matthew 10: 9–10.
(Literal translation from Aramaic)

In the Near East a traveling man is killed only when the bandits find money in his purse. This is done to hide the identity of the murderers in order to escape punishment. A man traveling without money has nothing to fear. If he should be in need and is met by robbers they will offer to help and let him go in

peace. Some highwaymen whose hospitality exceeds their vir-
tues would share their scanty supplies of food with travelers
whom they would meet, and in return they would relieve them
of their shoes, clothes or other articles which they need.

Many men would give all their wealth for the sake of having
their bodies healed, for their sight to be restored, or to have
their beloved ones raised from the dead. Jesus knew that His
disciples, endowed with the gift of healing, would soon accumu-
late riches and become the prey of the bandits and highwaymen
who might be tempted to kidnap them for ransom. Moreover,
the division of wealth among the disciples was soon to be a
problem and to stir rivalry and hatred which would weaken their
ranks and impair the progress of their work.

There were also grave fears that worldly men will offer themselves in the missionary cause of the Church, because of self-
interest.

Indeed, Jesus knew that the Eastern people would never
welcome and believe in the teachings of those who are paid for
preaching the word of God. His disciples were to be cared for
by the converts. They were worthy of their food.

When an employer hires a laborer, he bargains with him concerning wages and food. Customarily the Eastern people provide
food for all classes of labor but in the case of a laborer who is willing to work without wages, the question of food is not raised at
all by the employer. At the end the employer might also be willing
to pay a small wage. In this case even workers who are not good
workers often are employed just for their food. The Eastern laborer under any condition is assured of his food by his employer.

Looking Behind

"And Jesus said unto him, No man, having put his hand to the
plough, and looking back, is fit for the Kingdom of God."

St. Luke 9: 61–62.
(Literal translation from Aramaic)

A man who is considered an expert plougher and a good worker is one who while ploughing never looks behind. A new servant who has just been hired, is watched by his employer to see if he looks behind.

Ploughers who look behind are not considered good workers. They look behind to see how much of the field has been done in order to reckon when they will be finished. While doing this they have to stop the oxen.

A tireless plougher is one who always looks forward, determined to finish his work and only looks at the unploughed soil to see it decreasing in size.

The disciples of Jesus were not to look behind and be discouraged by the few converts which had been gained, because the work of the gospels at the outset was to progress very slowly. But they were to look forward to see the big work ahead.

Divorce

"And I say unto you, Whosoever shall put away his wife, except it be for fornication, and shall marry another, committeth adultery: and whoso marrieth her which is 'shvikta' (undivorced) does commit adultery."

St. Matthew 19: 9.
(Literal translation from Aramaic)

The Aramaic word "shvikta" means "an undivorced woman." A woman whose husband has not given her divorce papers. The Aramaic for divorced is "shrita," which means the one on whom the sacred bond has loosened.

The law of Moses permitted divorces on moral and criminal grounds. Nevertheless as the statutes of women in the East are inferior to those of men, men often tire of their wives and let them go but do not bother to obtain decrees of divorce. In this case, Jesus only condemned those who took advantage of the laxity of the law. He only attacked those who married women who were not actually divorced by law.

Good Master
"Malpana Tava"

"And there came one near and said unto him, 'Malpana Tava'—wonderful teacher—what good thing shall I do, that I may have eternal life?

"And he said unto him, Why do you call me wonderful? There is no one wonderful but one—God. But if you wish to enter into life, keep the commandments."

St. Matthew 19: 16–18.
(Literal translation from Aramaic)

The word "tava" in this case means wonderful. If the man had meant good or holy, he would have used the word "kadisha." "Tava" is used only when describing quality, such as wonderful carpenter, wonderful shepherd, wonderful ox. A shepherd may be a criminal, but still be called "good shepherd," not because of his good character, but because the sheep follow him, and he knows how to feed them. Jesus refused to accept the honor of the name "wonderful teacher," because an Easterner, whose teaching is from God, always tries to hide his popularity; the less he says concerning his knowledge, the more the people think of him; the more he hides himself, the more popular he becomes; but the Pharisees and scribes loved to be honored and called "wonderful rabbis."

Let the Dead Bury the Dead

"And another of his disciples said unto him, Lord suffer me first to go and bury my father.

"But Jesus said unto him, Follow me and let the dead bury their dead."

St. Matthew 8: 21, 22.

The Aramaic word for "dead" is "metta," and the word for "town" is "matta." There is a slight difference in pronunciation. In many of the mutilated manuscripts the small Aramaic character which determines the difference between the meaning of these two words is likely to be destroyed, especially in cases of carelessness in writing and because of the glas'sy manuscript ink used.

Jesus knew what this man meant. "Let me bury my father," if translated into English would mean: "My father is an old man, over seventy years of age. I have to support him until he dies." In the East when a man reaches this age, he is considered dead. He has finished his work and has no more interest in life. He can no longer earn and produce. He is a burden on the family. He entrusts everything to his oldest son, his first born; the son who is to continue his posterity. He has labored and toiled with the sweat of his brow, and raised his children. Now he expects them to take care of him. One often hears Easterners say: "My father is near the grave!" "My father is at the side of the grave." This, if literally translated into English would mean, "My father is dead and is put in the coffin, and the coffin is waiting beside the grave to be lowered." But the real meaning is, "My father may die any day. My father is very old; I expect him to pass away any time." If this man's father had been dead Jesus would not have been preaching that day. Instead He would have been one of the mourners until the dead man was buried.

It seems more likely that the early copyists and translators confused the word "matta" (town) for the word "metta" (dead) and what Jesus meant was, let the town bury the dead. This seems more reasonable because each town buries their own dead.

Say to No One

"And, behold, there came a leper and worshipped him, saying, Lord if thou wilt, thou canst make me clean.

"And Jesus put forth his hand, and touched him, saying, I will; be thou clean. And immediately his leprosy was cleansed.

"And Jesus saith unto him, See thou tell no man; but go thy way, shew thyself to the priest, and offer the gift that Moses commanded, for a testimony unto them."

St. Matthew 8: 2–5.

Jesus knew the psychology of the Eastern people. He knew that in those countries anything which is told secretly is published rapidly, being carried from mouth to mouth on the house tops. When a man tells his friend a secret he always says not to tell anyone. Therefore, the secret becomes public. If Jesus had told some of those men whom he healed to tell, they would have never told, because the act would not have been a secret and no one would have been interested to discuss it! On the other hand, the law of Moses demands that every man who is healed must show himself to the priests.

Two Women Grinding

Two women—a young girl and an old woman, sit down to grind wheat together, the young girl helps with one hand to turn the grinder and with the other she feeds the grinder. In the field two men work together—a boy and an old man. During the persecutions and wars when a town is conquered by the enemy the young girl at the house and the boy in the field are taken captive, but the old woman and old man are left.

Bearing a Pitcher of Water

"And he sendeth forth two of his disciples, and saith unto them, Go ye into the city, and there shall meet you a man bearing a pitcher of water: follow him."

St. Mark 14: 13.

In Palestine and Mesopotamia, water is only carried by women. For men to carry water would be considered effeminate, even were they suffering from thirst. However, as the women are not allowed to be employed in public places, keepers of lodging houses are obliged to hire male servants to perform this task of carrying water. It is customary in the East for relatives and friends to entertain each other when traveling. This decreases the demand for lodging houses. In some of the large cities, however, there is usually one or two public places, chiefly for native unmarried travelers and foreign merchants of a different creed, who are not welcome to stay over night in a family home.

Jesus instructed his disciples to follow the man who bore the pitcher of water because that was the easiest way for them to find a lodging house in a city like Jerusalem, where streets were irregularly laid out, with no names and numbers.

Eli, Eli, Lmana Sabachthani

"My God, My God, for this I was kept."

"Now from the sixth hour there was darkness over all the land unto the ninth hour.

"And about the ninth hour Jesus cried with a loud voice, saying, Eli, Eli, lmana sabachthani.

"Some of them that stood there, when they heard that, said, This man calleth for Elias."

Matt. 27: 45–47.

All versions of the Gospels have retained these words in the original tongue and given them a different meaning. Matthew, according to Eastern version, does not translate them, because he wrote to the people who had seen Jesus and heard Him preaching. It also seems probable that the later writers did not agree on its exact meaning when they translated them into Greek. This term even at present is only used by the Aramaic-speaking people in Assyria, the same language which the Galileans spoke at the time of our Lord. This phrase in Aramaic means, "My God, my God, for this I was kept. (this was my destiny—I was born for this)."

Jesus did not quote the Psalms. If He had He would have said these words in Hebrew instead of Aramaic, and if He had translated them from Hebrew He would have used the Aramaic word "nashatani," which means "forsaken me," instead of the word "shabacktani," which in this case means, "kept me." Even the soldiers who stood by the cross did not understand what Jesus said in that hour of agony and suffering. They thought that He was calling on Elijah because the word Elijah in Aramaic is "Elia," which is similar to that for God, "Eli."

In those last minutes of suffering Jesus watched the crowd, which was composed of Rabbis, Priests, men and women of Jerusalem, who had come up to watch Him dying. Some insulted Him. Others spitting in His face, and others calling Him names and challenging his claim that He is a man of God but instead that he was a malefactor and sinner. Jesus only made a statement to Himself and to the friends who were also standing and hiding in the crowds near the Cross. That He was born for that hour that He may bear witness to the truth and open the way for the others who were to be crucified—that that was His destiny. That there was nothing else that could have given such a glorious victory as the Cross.

The disciples and women who were from Galilee never for a moment could have thought that Jesus said that God had forsaken Him. How could He say that when He had told His disciples that the whole world would forsake Him, even they, but that the Father would be with Him. When he told Peter that if He wished He could bring angels to fight for Him, and when He said, "Father, let it be Thy wish if I should drink this cup." These words, "Eli, Eli, lmana sabachthani," even today are used by Assyrians when they suffer and die unjustly. Instead of com-

Some Examples of the Usage
of Aramaic Words

The reader must know how the words are used in each case.

SHAA	Time
	Clock
	Turn

NAPHSHA	Person
	Life
	Body
	Soul

BARNASHA	Man
	Mankind
	Son of man
	Might happen

KAM	To stand up
	To arise from the grave
	To become a ruler
	To arise in fortunes

ROOKHA	Holy Ghost
	Spirit
	Wind
	Life
	Rheumatism
	In Spirits Prophecy
	Soul